minimalism room by room

minimalism room by room

a customized plan to declutter your home & simplify your life

Elizabeth Enright Phillips

ROCKRIDGE
PRESS

For general information on our other products and services or to obtain technical support, please contact our Customer Care Department within the U.S. at (866) 744-2665, or outside the U.S. at (510) 253-0500.

Rockridge Press publishes its books in a variety of electronic and print formats. Some content that appears in print may not be available in electronic books, and vice versa.

TRADEMARKS: Rockridge Press and the Rockridge Press logo are trademarks or registered trademarks of Callisto Media Inc. and/or its affiliates, in the United States and other countries, and may not be used without written permission. All other trademarks are the property of their respective owners. Rockridge Press is not associated with any product or vendor mentioned in this book.

Interior and Cover Designer: Jami Spittler
Photo Art Director/Art Manager: Sue Bischofberger
Editor: Claire Yee
Production Editor: Ashley Polikoff
Photography: © Ogovorka/shutterstock, cover; © MAX BLENDER 3D/shutterstock, cover; © New Africa/shutterstock, cover and p. 56; © Followtheflow/shutterstock, p. ii; © KatarzynaBialasiewicz/iStock, pp. vi and 162; © Gladiathor/iStock, p. viii; © Photographee.eu/shutterstock, pp. xiv, 82, 146, and 170; © ImageFlow/shutterstock, p. 8; © asbe/iStock, p. 38; © united photo studio/shutterstock, p. 103; © Zastolskiy Victor/shutterstock, p. 104; and © nurulanga/iStock, p. 124.
Author photo courtesy of Running Creek Design.

ISBN: Print 978-1-64152-967-9
eBook 978-1-64152-968-6

R1

To my father, Kenneth Enright.
You showed me what valuing people
over stuff truly meant.

To my love, Kurt. Always.

Contents

The Beauty of Less

What if you could walk into a beautiful, peaceful house, containing simple, useful items, and have it be your own home? What if your bank account reflected the increased savings of having fewer expenses? Does an emotional weight lift off your shoulders at the possibilities? Maybe you're ready to shed the load and excess of materialism.

Contrary to the cultural norms of "bigger is always better," the minimalist concept of "less" can be the better choice. The minimalist stereotype of high design and stark empty rooms isn't the only form of minimalism. It's time to dream a little about what "the beauty of less" looks like for you!

For me, minimalism looks like a little log home in the woods with a front porch swing. Our home works for our family and is filled with simple, useful, and beautiful items that serve us—not the other way around. But it wasn't always this way!

I remember vividly how piles of useful items would choke out my ability to see the beauty around me. I felt waves of hopelessness as I sorted through endless plastic tubs in the basement of the duplex where I began my decluttering journey. I was drowning in stuff, and our finances were a mess. I had walked away from a full ride to the grad school of my dreams and left my corporate job, having made the choice to be home to care for our newborn daughter due to her unforeseen medical condition. At the time, I didn't realize how cluttered my home was until I faced the reality all day—I couldn't safely walk in our back door due to all the boxes, bags, and random garden tools stacked high. I don't like to admit it, but the dirty dishes almost reached the ceiling!

I felt the deep-soul conviction to "get my house in order." Amid my own mess, this simple thought motivated me to make a massive change in my own thinking and my own home. I decided to start decluttering and over the next several years ended up donating 560-plus huge bags of previously important items to charity. I knew we couldn't replace anything I donated, but I was willing to risk making mistakes in order to simplify my house.

Money was tight. In fact, we were broke. We weren't making ends meet without my salary and health insurance, which we desperately needed with a sick baby. My colleagues said, "You can't afford to leave the department!" My family said, "You have a good secure job!" Yet I knew in my heart I made the right choice to care for our daughter, and I didn't want to leave chaos in my house as a legacy. I knew I desperately needed less:

Less clutter because I aspired to have visually clean and well-designed spaces and struggled with postpartum depression exacerbated by guilt and visual clutter around me.

Less stuff to cause trip-and-fall hazards because I'm clumsy.

Less money wasted because I was completely broke and needed to stop buying as a form of emotional control.

Today, I wake up to a life that I love. As a financial and minimalist coach, I support people who are ready to create simplicity in their homes and stability in their finances. I built my business according to a schedule that I laid out for myself, so I am able to provide vital services to my private clients locally and around the globe and still homeschool my children.

The "stuff" part is easy to grasp. Many of us have too much stuff. Yet, you may wonder, how does money fit into minimalism? Is there a monetary benefit to minimalism? Consider this scenario: When your kitchen is cluttered and you can't find the right tools, you're less likely to want to cook in it—but you're hungry, so you order takeout. A simpler life means you'll enjoy cooking in your simple kitchen and order out less frequently, saving money. It also means you don't buy a second (or third) bag of flour because you can't find the other two in all the mess. Minimalism results in smarter spending across your entire lifestyle—whether that means eliminating cable and canceling unused subscriptions or simply discontinuing spontaneous shopping habits in exchange for new, more enriching choices.

Let me illustrate, in a small way, the emotional benefit of minimalism. In a client meeting, one overwhelmed mompreneur sobbed with joy at her newfound ability to cook with her toddler in her simplified kitchen. She was surprised to find that *less* clutter actually gave her *more* of what she truly wanted—quality bonding time. Another client was able to clear away years of clutter (and the associated discouragement) in order to fill out her student loan forgiveness documents. She was able to choose less and finally make space for that important task . As a result, she was able to start building her dream life with a fresh outlook.

In the process of choosing less, we find more: more hope, more authenticity, more freedom, more opportunities to serve, and more connection to those we love and to our larger communities.

Imagine the freedom that comes from simply believing that less is possible. You can begin to choose less, regardless of what others say! You can choose to no longer be burdened by the trap of comparing your home to others'. Choose less—one step, one cupboard, one room at a time. You can rewrite the story of what home is for you and perhaps, in the process, rewrite your entire life.

How to Use This Book

This book is the guide I wish existed when I was drowning in mountains of stuff. Throughout these pages are simple steps to start decluttering your own spaces. This book is structured as a room-by-room guide so you can make progress at your own pace. Instead of being overwhelmed by decluttering an entire house, you'll learn to tackle smaller, short-term projects as you make your way through your home.

Some of the rooms addressed in this book may not be applicable to you, so feel free to skip around to what's in your unique situation after reading through chapter 1. If you're decluttering one specific room, this resource will give you the tools to accomplish your goal. If you have your eye on the entire house, I'll show you where to start and help you plan your tasks throughout each space. The book begins with the easiest spaces first and works toward more challenging spaces as a progression.

You'll find tales of success and hope in real-life stories in this book. I'd like you to chronicle your own journey, too, so grab a notebook or journal. Even though this is a systematic book, I know that each situation has its own obstacles and everyone's journey is a little different. You'll want to take notes for your own situation in your Decluttering Journal. Journaling is a powerful tool that can open up new mental pathways, reveal new opportunities, and change your mind-set. It's also a great way to look back and marvel at the transformation.

I've also included charts and a variety of other tools to guide you through the emotional and physical rough spots. This book is a resource you can run back to as needed, and your journal will chronicle your progress. You're always welcome to come back to my front porch swing, have another cup of tea, and start again with grace and a new plan of action.

Exercise: Let's Get Prepared!

There are a few steps I'd like for you to take to prepare for this journey of less:

Get a journal. Don't skip this! It's tempting to skip right ahead to the chapter on the room that frustrates you most. Get a journal first. Make a solid decision to journal this process and find a notebook now. I personally use both a composition book and Google Docs for its voice-to-text feature on the app. I also highly recommend creating a photo journal of your progress. I use a Google Photos album for "before and after" pictures.

Create a reminder in your calendar. To make decluttering a priority and to check that you've given yourself enough time to do so, set all your decluttering dates on your paper or digital calendar. You may need to eliminate any unnecessary appointments or commitments.

Start dreaming! What would you do with the rest of your life if time and money weren't considerations? What if you didn't have so much stuff to maintain? I always start here with my clients, even if their goals don't seem attainable right now. The goal of minimalism is not to live in a perfect house; it's to live an intentional life. What does your best life look like? Take 10 minutes here to begin crafting that vision. Write down your ideas in your Decluttering Journal as your first entry.

ONE

The Minimalist Lifestyle

"Letting go of
physical clutter also
declutters mind
and soul."

—UNKNOWN

I didn't grow up minimalist. I am a "saver" and associate items with sentiment and memories. I understand that you might be nervous about what minimalism entails, but rest knowing that you can craft a path that works for you.

There's More to Minimalism Than Meets the Eye

When you hear the word "minimalism," maybe you think of stark interiors that are all white, cold, and uninviting. Maybe you remember the term from an art history class. However, the new concept of minimalism, which has grown over the last several decades, is about creating an intentionally simpler lifestyle with fewer material possessions.

You might have heard about minimalism but aren't ready to fully embrace it. Just imagine one room or space in your home and think about how it can be improved. I want you to imagine feeling a weight lifted off your shoulders when you walk into your kitchen and sigh with relief that everything is clean and ready for a new meal. I want you to experience increased clarity and mental focus when you sit down at your desk, having all you need to complete vital tasks quickly. Even the smallest changes can provide tremendous benefits.

I had one client who had a wall of cardboard boxes filled with sentimental papers, journals, and memorabilia lining her hallway. She sought my help. Together, we mapped out a plan. She chose to tackle one box first. She found that the open space made it easier to move down the hallway, so she sorted another box. The day all the boxes were gone, she exclaimed, "I am no longer climbing over a wall of past memories to get out the door!"

As this client sorted and processed the items associated with her past, she was able to embrace her current season and look forward with increased hope for the future. What started with one small change provided exponential benefits. It cleared space for her children to play and made it easier to move down the hallway. Best of all, she experienced emotional release from the pressure of saving all the items.

Why Choose Minimalism?

As I've worked with clients and their families to integrate minimalism into their lifestyle, I've encountered many skeptics. One gentleman asked, "Why, after working hard to purchase material goods, would I simply give them away?" It's a valid question, but the benefits of minimalism far outweigh monetary numbers. They include:

- Saving money (by eliminating unnecessary expenses)
- Less maintenance
- Less visual and mental clutter
- A more environmentally sustainable lifestyle
- More time for experiences and travel (I can now pack my six kids for vacation and get out the door in an hour!)
- A deeper connection with people rather than stuff
- Release from fear and scarcity mind-sets
- A deeper sense of community and generosity
- Moving beyond self-centered living to serving others

Each household's parameters for minimalism will invariably be different. My Facebook group, Frugal Minimalists, has more than 89,000 members from around the world who integrate minimalism within their own diverse cultures. Still, minimalists share core values that unite and guide our purchasing choices and streamline our lives. Minimalism isn't merely an interior design style; it's a lifestyle that you can craft for yourself, and you'll find camaraderie and idea-sharing among this growing number of people who are also choosing the lifestyle of less.

Minimalism has been criticized as being only for those who can afford to replace items that may be donated by mistake. Some people even propose that minimalism will provide an empty life. The irony of writing a book about decluttering is not lost on me when I struggled to declutter books! At one time, I would have argued that I didn't have money to replace the items I donated and later needed. In the midst of all these valid questions, I found answers. I realized that the principle of reciprocal generosity more than compensated for my mistakes. Those who are generous to others feel better and receive generosity in return. And, in the rare instance I made a mistake in eliminating an item I needed later, I was able to find a replacement for free or at a low cost. My life is much fuller and focused more on generosity because of minimalism, rather than worrying about finding affordable replacements.

I want to be clear—our physical items aren't inherently evil. We all need a place to sleep, eat, work, and enjoy our lives. A desire for beauty and even luxury is not morally wrong. The problem stems from our consumer-minded culture shoving every kind of product, gadget, or trinket down our throat to the point of overconsumption. This overconsumption has serious implications not just in terms of complicating our own lives, as this book explores, but also in terms of how people are treated in the production process and the environmental impact of the materials sourced.

Simplicity and Sustainability

Choosing minimalism daily and living in environmentally conscious ways speaks volumes to the next generation about how people are more valuable than stuff. As we discuss the benefits of minimalism, we see the positive impact of intentional living spread in every direction, including how we treat the resources of our planet. Mindless consumption is impacting our environment by depleting our natural resources in unprecedented ways. In my minimalist journey, I discovered a renewed passion for environmental sustainability. The impact of human consumption on our oceans, water, air, and soil is staggering. Trash that cannot be recycled, reused, or rotted becomes pollution. When my husband and I switched over to a minimalist lifestyle, we saw a direct correlation between this choice and the amount of trash we produced. We took a year to study zero-waste concepts as we decluttered and were able to recycle or eliminate 80 percent of our previous trash production! We were also able to initially work our monthly budget down by 20 percent, and eventually down by 45 percent. Less waste and less money spent equaled more money saved and reallocated wisely. Money-saving and environmental choices often work together within the minimalist home.

To that end, I've included sustainability tips throughout this book that provide easy ways to implement this into your lifestyle.

One Room at a Time

Why adopt minimalism on a room-by-room basis? The best way to tackle an enormous task is to break it down into manageable, bite-size pieces. Remember, we'll start with the easiest rooms and spaces. This will allow you to experiment with what works best for you. You're welcome to try new ideas, take risks, and even fail. I've certainly failed often! The important part is to learn what works and doesn't work for you. Each room you work on will teach you more about yourself and your household.

Each chapter begins with a helpful section called "Where to Start?" Often, my clients feel overwhelmed when faced with the many areas to declutter, but when we take it step by step and room by room, they can begin to see how to bring order and simplicity to their home.

One of my clients decided to focus on creating spaces of rest. She faced a daily one-way 90-minute commute and realized she needed a safe haven to come home to. This determined which rooms she focused on first: the entryway and bedroom.

What do *you* need? Pull out your Decluttering Journal and think about which areas create the most stress or strife in your home. Close your eyes and make a mental map. Think about the ways that family members, friends, and pets come and go. To envision how your household flows, picture a pathway of footprints going from the entrance and throughout the house. Natural flow is important and can easily be disrupted.

When I first started decluttering, I wanted to do the whole house in a weekend. While that might be possible for some households, for me, as a mom with small children and a business to run, moving fast proved a disaster—I made my house worse instead of better. Going room by room will help you avoid disrupting the actual flow of your household and will instead gently redirect its natural path.

Together we'll tackle the spaces that make the most impact in the least amount of time, and we'll clear areas that cause you frustration. You'll also find money-saving tips, feelings checklists, and affirmation statements throughout the book to help you through this!

Affirmation Statements

I will defeat the clutter.

I am bringing healing and peace to my home.

I may make mistakes, but I am always learning and growing.

TWO

Entryway, Bathrooms, and Communal Closets

"If you talk about it,
it's a dream; if you
envision it, it's possible;
but if you schedule it,
it's real."

—TONY ROBBINS

In any decluttering journey, it helps to have a starting point that will help immediately with daily household activities. Make a decluttering date on the calendar to get started.

Where to Start?

Start at the beginning: your entryway door. Step outside, take a deep breath, and then come back in again. Look around. Is it easy to come and go in this space? I want you to think in terms of what I call your "Go Routine," or simply your high-traffic areas. In any house-hold, people need to be able to come and go easily and peacefully. We'll tackle these high-traffic spaces first:

- Entryway
- Bathrooms
- Coat closets
- Linen closets

Questions to Ask

In each of your high-traffic areas, look around and ask yourself these questions:

- Do I have a designated place for the items that are supposed to go here?
- Where do my necessary items go each time?
- Where do coats go?
- Where do other people's items go? Is there a space for guests or other household members? Pet items?
- What categories of items are hiding in that pile of clutter?
- What material is the clutter made of? Fabric? Paper? Plastic?

- Can I access the most necessary things quickly?
- What items are supposed to "live" in this particular spot? What's here that shouldn't be?

I could never find my purse, keys, or wallet, but I never stopped to ask myself why I would put it in any of 16 different places each time I came home. There wasn't an open space for me to dedicate a place for my necessary items. I couldn't even shut the coat closet door because shoes, rakes, and extra garden hoses attacked me if I tried. The bathroom linen closet was a waiting avalanche of mismatched blankets, towels, and sheets, so I couldn't find anything quickly. If this has happened to you, it's time to schedule a "Simplicity Self-Care Date."

This is how it worked for me: I set aside a short period of time twice a day, usually when my kids were asleep, to declutter my target area or room. I devoted 15 minutes in the morning and 10 minutes in the evening. I called it my "Simplicity Self-Care Date" because I knew I needed to make this a serious, written-in-pen-on-the-calendar priority.

Another way to carve out decluttering time is to do "Quantum Sprints." This is a planned, full-out decluttering attack on the problem areas. It requires setting aside a large chunk of time and sticking with it. Maybe it's the same day as trash and recycling pickup or charity donation pickup. You may need to take a vacation day or a full weekend to declutter.

I recommend doing a combination of Simplicity Self-Care Dates and Quantum Sprints to get the best results and create permanent change. I know it's hard to find time. Maybe you're a caregiver, or juggling a high-pressure career and life, or building a business from scratch, or all of the above! No matter your story, finding time to declutter starts with a mental shift. Trust that taking the time to declutter will help you go faster in every other area of your life.

Finding Time to Declutter

Set your decluttering appointments in stone like any vital appointment. Next, make a timeline with solid begin/end dates just like any
professional project. Lay out specific goals within those dates on
the calendar. Even if you don't stick exactly to it, marking it on your
calendar, and even sharing the news of your plans with your loved
ones, will help keep your progress going.

Sorting and Logistics

Now let's dive into the four-step process for sorting and disposing of
the clutter. The steps will be similar across each room, but the decisions may be slightly different and require various action steps. You
can use the same process in each room to work systematically.

Step 1: The First Pass

Timer Set: 15 to 30 minutes per area

Materials Needed

2 heavy-duty 30-gallon garbage bags (one for trash,
one for donations)

1 clear plastic tub (Delivery Tub)

Recycling Tub

Decluttering Journal

Decluttering Chart (page 173)

Pen

Phone for "before" photos

Turn off your phone notifications at this time. I know you *think* you won't look at those notifications. I thought that, too, but five hours later, I was still on Pinterest and had nothing accomplished. But before you put your phone down, snap a quick "before" photo—you'll enjoy seeing your progress later.

Grab everything that you know is trash and place it in the first garbage bag. Throw anything recyclable in the Recycling Tub. If you're not sure whether to trash it, you are welcome to save it in your plastic tub. You might want to "thank" the item for its service (as organizing consultant Marie Kondo suggests). If you can't recycle it easily, I want you to release it without environmental guilt. Letting go of the past is key. Be at peace with your decisions, knowing that you are creating a new life where you won't create as much trash in the future.

As you eliminate items from this space, you might find it helpful to use the Decluttering Chart (page 173). This chart contains 500 squares, and you'll mark an X in one box for each item that is either donated, sold, recycled, or thrown away.

The clear Delivery Tub is for items you want to keep that don't belong in this location.

If you see items that you know will go to charity, toss them quickly into the second garbage bag and label it your donation bag.

At the end of this quick sort, you may be feeling energized. You may be tempted to try to tackle your entire house right this second. Resist the urge. Instead, stop decluttering while you still have energy and take the trash and recycling out. Put the donation bag in your vehicle or on your front porch and, if ready, call to schedule a pickup from your local charity. Finally, take the Delivery Tub and deliver it to the general area where the items are used so you can at least close the lid to the tub.

If you still have time, set 5 to 10 minutes on the timer for delivering your Delivery Tub items to their proper place. The timer will help you move quickly and not get distracted. Don't worry if the items don't totally fit in the area where they will go. You'll work your way to those spaces in future chapters. Close is good enough.

WARNING: OBSTACLE AHEAD!

Don't attempt to do a deep clean while you are trying to declutter. This is a marathon, not a sprint. I've made this mistake more than once. This is not the time to scrub every nook and cranny of your house. You can do a quick wipe of the area where you're decluttering, but stop there. Once the area is completely decluttered, you can come back and do a deep clean.

Next, you're going to set up a Decluttering Command Center. Designate a space that you won't trip over but is easily accessible, such as the top shelf of your newly cleared closet. Leave your Delivery Tub, Decluttering Journal, Decluttering Chart, and trash bags there— you'll need these later.

Here's the best part now that you've completed step 1: It's time to give yourself a reward! One key concept is to make sure that you reward yourself consistently. Have a cup of tea, take a walk in nature, enjoy some sunshine, play with your kids or your puppies, do yoga, pray quietly, or make that long-overdue phone call to a loved one or friend. Celebrate your progress by doing activities that feed your soul.

This is one of the most important parts of decluttering, because you'll need to feel that your labor has been worth it. Rewards can help you stay motivated and refreshed from the hard work that's involved in decluttering. Rewards will keep the process fun and are a way to involve other household members as you work through communal spaces in coming chapters.

Next, grab your calendar and schedule another session, either later in the afternoon or tomorrow morning when you can tackle step 2. Set a reminder on your phone. Try to set this time for no longer than a couple days later while your thoughts about these spaces are still fresh in your mind.

Step 2: The Big Sort

Timer Set: 20 to 30 minutes per session with multiple sessions

Materials Needed

1 trash bag for trash

1 trash bag for donating

Recycling Tub

1 plastic Sell Tub for items that can be sold

1 plastic tub for items to be given away to specific people

1 to 4 plastic Delivery Tubs for other locations in your home

Decluttering Journal and pen

Decluttering Chart (page 173)

Labeling supplies

Resist the temptation to phone a friend or family member when decluttering! It can slow your progress. Instead, check out an inspiring podcast or upbeat music to keep you focused and encouraged.

Step 2 will take more time than step 1. You may even need to repeat this step anywhere from two to 10 times. Don't despair if this takes longer than you expect. In this step, you're going to sort through the items that you've kept in your target areas of entryway, bath, and closets. Sort these objects into categories. The first two categories are Keep and Donate. Later, as you go back through your Keep items, you may determine that more items can be donated. Group like items together, such as coats, belts, hats, and linens, so you can take an accurate assessment of your household needs.

Decluttering Emotions 101

Many family members feel stressed when first starting a decluttering journey. Here are some important tips:

- Do this phase of decluttering alone.
- If applicable, don't touch your partner's personal items. Leave those alone as much as possible.
- Establish a mind-set that you will avoid angry cleaning and blaming, especially if money is tight and you're upset by items in these spaces that family members have purchased but not used. ▶

> • Include the members of your household later in a relaxed but official family meeting, not while decluttering. Don't burn bridges with expectations or accusations. In a calm moment, maybe after a quiet dinner, begin by asking the right questions, which might include:
>   • How can we set up this space to make life easier?
>   • What do you think about how this room is working?
>   • Do you have any ideas for improving this space?

Assigning Jobs to Your Spaces

It helps to think about the job each space does, and to do that, you'll assign a job to each one. Take out your journal and jot some notes. For example, here are the jobs my entryway performs:

- Stores shoes
- Stores coats
- Holds the household calendar (zero-waste chalkboard calendar)
- Processes trash/recycling/compost
- Holds items that need to "go," such as library books and items that need to be returned to other people or stores—I call this my "Go-Shelf"

You may journal about the jobs of each closet. What should ideally be kept in each closet for your household? Make a list. It may look like this:

Entryway Closet

- Grill tools
- Shoes
- Winter hats/gloves

- Boots
- Coats
- Umbrella

Think of your spaces as "employees" of your house. How is this space "working" for you? What is its job? Are you setting this space up for success, just like you would an actual employee? You may want to temporarily label the areas as you are sorting. This could mean taping labels to shelves. My husband used to joke that he feared waking up with the word "husband" written across his forehead! It was a valid concern—I labeled almost everything. I used a washable crayon to write on closet shelves to visualize and remember what category of items I wanted to put there.

Once you know the jobs of each space, you'll know what items belong, what you need, and what you should get rid of. Do you need a bench for putting on shoes? Do you have enough sturdy coat hangers to match the number of coats you hang? Place any extras into your Delivery Tub for now. You may need to use them elsewhere. The key is to keep only what is essential for this space to do its job right now.

In your journal, write down any patterns and categories that you are beginning to see. Here, journaling will show you how you normally use this space. Do pantry items end up getting left in the entryway? Are you trying to shove garden tools into the coat closet because you don't have outside storage? (That was me!) Once you identify these problem areas by categories, you can start to think through solutions. Don't worry if you don't know the solution yet;

just focus on finding the patterns—you'll discover solutions as you continue to declutter.

Since you're going through many more items in step 2, you'll need several Delivery Tubs. You can choose to label them like I do:

- To go basement
- To go outside
- To go [other places in the house] (you may label this "bathroom," "master bedroom," etc.)

You'll also need another large tub for items to sell. You may want to tape a paper copy of your Tracking Sheet for Items to Sell (page 178) inside the tub lid. You'll be documenting the items on this sheet.

Here's a place to be honest with yourself. If it's winter and you live at the North Pole, you may want to donate these duplicate garden tools rather than try to sell them for $5. Consider whether it's worth your time to sell.

Step 3: Deliver/Sell/Donate

Keep each session in the manageable range of 15 to 30 minutes, because all the decision-making can tax your brain. You're making great progress, and you want to pace yourself. Avoid my mistakes! I would declutter for an entire day, delivering, selling, and donating, and then not touch anything for two weeks because I was exhausted. Take your time. Go back to the Delivery Tubs. This is a perfect opportunity to recruit children, your own or neighborhood kids who are ready for a job and a treat, as your "delivery drivers" between rooms.

Send out your delivery items to their respective zones. Don't worry if the items don't all fit in the zone; close is good enough. However, if the items need to go outside to a storage shed, take them all the way. Don't leave them on the porch like I used to do. If you've got kid helpers, make a game out of this with music and a timer. Do it quickly and with enthusiasm!

Next, set up the items that need to be sold. I recommend simply starting on Facebook Marketplace or local buy/sell/trade groups. You can also post these items on your personal Facebook page and list the items in your comments. Set a limited amount of time for the items to sell—seven days is plenty. If the items don't sell within that period of time, donate them immediately.

The other trash bag is for donations. This may include outgrown shoes, winter coats, or extra purses, all of which you can donate to a charity (see ideas for where to donate on page 184). Maybe you've got five extra blankets shoved in the back of your linen closet. A great place to donate extra blankets is to a local homeless shelter. I took my children along, and it was an impactful experience donating blankets we no longer used. What had been clutter and used-up space in our linen closet became critical warmth to those in need.

MONEY-SAVING TIP:

Many of these donations are tax-deductible. Ask for a tax receipt from the charity that you donate to and make a quick list of the items. Put the list in your tax file for next year. (Don't worry, we're headed to your office next.) Refer to www.irs.gov/taxtopics/tc506 for guidelines on charitable donations.

Step 4: Tracking and Celebrating

Try to create a positive tone when it comes to tracking your progress. Use your Decluttering Chart (page 173) and make it a game! Set a goal for the number of items to remove from a particular space, plus a reward for reaching the goal. The stress and mental pressure from the clutter will diminish with every item you sell or donate.

Some people may experience an undercurrent of grief when decluttering and struggle to find joy in the process. This is especially true for those of us who grew up in poverty or had significant trauma surrounding finances. Finding that positive mental space starts with the language we use in our minds as we track and celebrate our progress.

Questions to Ask

Think through the following questions in your decluttering progress. Be careful to keep it positive:

- "How can I make more room in the entryway or bathroom for items that I need?"
- "What would help me the most in this space?"
- "Do I need more space for this item?"
- "I want to feel peaceful when I/we come in the door. How do we do that?"
- "How can I help make this space peace-filled?"

Avoid critical questions (to yourself or others) such as, "Why do you spend so much money on junk you don't use?"

I've included a Tracking Sheet for Items to Sell (page 178) as a spreadsheet for any sold items. This sheet contains columns to list the type of item, the platform it's listed on, and the asking price. Once the items are sold, put the money into a separate savings account. Use this money for something the whole household can enjoy.

Saying Goodbye to Stuff

As you are decluttering the entryway, the communal closets, and the bathroom, look at the pathways between those spaces. These areas are high-traffic spots in all households. Let's clear those pathways!

Entryway: Items to Discard/Recycle

- Coupons/ads/unopened junk mail
- Newspapers or magazines
- Broken umbrellas or other items
- Ripped raincoats or Windbreakers
- Unused plastic water bottles
- Old keys and key rings

MONEY-SAVING TIP:
Cancel any newspaper and magazine subscriptions you're not actively reading. Try using the library periodical section instead. Many libraries offer digital access for added convenience.

Closet Items to Discard:

- Shoe boxes
- Ripped, stained linens (you can save and cut up a few to use as rags, but set a limit of 10)

- Old shoes that cannot be repaired
- Broken coat hangers
- Unused appliances, mini-carpet shampooer items
- Incomplete items needing repair
- Incomplete DIY projects

Bathroom Items to Discard:

- Old bottles of unused or partially used shampoo (donate unopened ones you won't use and trash the rest)
- Outdated makeup
- Outdated personal care items or medications
- Unused appliances, water picks, curling irons, and humidifiers

Getting Past the "Perceived Value" Mentality

A big tripping point in decluttering is any item with "perceived value." If money was spent on the item, it tends to have more value placed upon it, regardless of its actual resale worth. But there is also a hidden cost to these items: the extra storage needed to keep them, and the mental cost and guilt for having them but never using them. Discarding or donating items with perceived value may actually save money in the long run. Items in need of repair can be released to someone who can fix them, and you won't need to pay for the repair. Perhaps you need to decide that it's not fixable for you at this season. I know you want to be a good steward of the world's resources, but sometimes it's time to just let go.

I struggled with getting rid of items that I bought but never used, but eventually came to a place in my life where I could release an item without psychological waves of guilt. I told myself, "I made the best decision in that moment and learned from it. I'm moving forward and will make a different decision next time. I refuse to carry this guilt anymore!"

It's time to live light and forgive the past: past purchases, past decisions, and past shame.

Affirmation Statements (*when saying goodbye to items*)

I made the best decision I could have in that moment, and I've learned.

I'm moving forward to a new future.

I'm making new choices.

I won't carry guilt anymore.

I am worthy of a fresh start.

It's time to forgive yourself! Maybe you need to say it out loud. I had to say it aloud and change my inner dialogue, especially when I was surrounded by hundreds of boxes. Copy these affirmations in your journal or record them into your phone to remind yourself that you're on your way to a fresh start.

Minimalist Concept
Decluttering is always about forgiveness.

Own Less, Live More

I acknowledge there is risk involved in any sort of change, and decluttering is no exception. I often feared I would get rid of something I would need later. In fact, I have donated or thrown away items I wound up needing later. I quickly found a solution to those situations by looking for multiuse items, borrowing the item, or buying an upgrade of the item on sale. I learned that the fear of this risk was unfounded, and I trusted myself to make good decisions on what to keep and what to donate. If you've struggled with the fear that you'll need the item later, it's time to take a bit of risk in learning discernment (what to keep/discard) and creativity (resilience when given limitations). By risking making the wrong decision, you'll learn discernment of what to keep and of what is a good decision for your household. By believing and practicing resilience, you'll learn to see multiple uses for common items and know what you actually need.

To a great extent, this process is about learning to trust your decision-making in choosing to own less and live more authentically. A recent client learned that she needed to speak up to her spouse about his purchases of what she felt were nonessential items. She felt relief in being authentic to her beliefs and honest about her opinions while communicating both in a loving way. Another client realized that the sheer number of shoes in her household made it impossible for her girls to find the correct matching ones. She placed a limit by determining a number of shoes to be worn per season and per child. Her girls had no trouble deciding on and finding their shoes. Limits don't need to be constricting—they can actually provide more freedom within a set framework.

The benefits of a clean bathroom and organized closets primarily surround ease of use, but they can also help you save money. How often have you bought bar soap only to find you have two other multipacks sitting behind all the clutter? Being able to see what supplies you have and what needs replacing can save money by eliminating the purchase of duplicate items.

MONEY-SAVING TIP:

Write the date opened on hygiene products, such as liquid soap, shampoo, or lotion, to chart how long each product lasts. Use that information to purchase enough (but not too much) when those items come on sale, knowing you can use them before the expiration date.

Feelings Checklist

Saying goodbye to items can stir up grief or trigger waves of emotion. Let's name these emotions and process them.

Take your journal and list your thoughts with a short explanation so you can identify what is coming up for you in this moment. The most important step after identifying the emotion is to take charge of it. The key is to grow into your new life: one emotion, one thought, one step, one donation bag at a time!

Here are some examples of what you might feel and some explanations behind those emotions:

Relief: Dang, I'm glad that's all finally gone!

Fear: What if [insert beloved family member name] finds out I gave that away?

Accomplished: I'm so glad I'm done with this!

Nervous: What if I need something I just gave away but don't have money to buy it again? ▶

▶ Excited: Let's see if this minimalism thing really works!

Grief: I feel the loss of familiarity, even if it was a familiar mess.

Happiness: I'm so happy to live in the peace of this newly redone space.

Disgust: Why did I have so much, and why did it take me so long to do this?

Frustration: It's still not quite what I wanted because others aren't on board.

Surprise: I can't believe we had this much stuff.

Anger: I am upset with myself that I let it get this bad.

Joy: Wow, it looks like a whole new space.

Hope: I'm really going to conquer this mess!

Unworthy: I can't even imagine a clean, clear space—that's just for rich folks, and it's not really me.

Jittery: I think I've given away too much and I need to go shopping.

Use this list as a starting point for your own emotions and explanations. It can help you learn more about yourself, what drives you, and what you can work on.

Reimagining Your Space

Now comes the fun part—redesigning your fresh new canvas of a space! Chart the room out on graph paper or use an online floor-planning tool. Whatever method you choose, be sure to measure and include the amount of square footage a door needs to fully open. Let's take this design process step by step as well.

Step 1: Clear the walls and all surfaces. Clear the walls and shelves of any remaining decorative items that may have escaped your notice during decluttering. This will help you see which elements are your favorites. Remember and repeat this four-step process with decorative items if needed:

- The First Pass
- The Big Sort
- Deliver/Sell/Donate
- Tracking and Celebrating

Step 2: Shop the house first! Don't worry if something is typically a bath item but looks better in the entryway. Reject traditional design rules that don't apply to you or your newly decluttered space. Some rules will work well, such as raising your curtain rods above the window frames for high-ceiling rooms with small windows. But you can also remove window coverings altogether and hang up white twin bed sheets with safety pins like I did for five years until I found the exact look I wanted!

Step 3: Create a focal point. When you walk into the entryway or bathroom, what's the first thing you see? Where do your eyes come to rest? I like to use consistent neutral colors to offset the pine-colored walls of our log home. Your home may need a vibrant color. Your focal point may not be a masterpiece per se, but you'll want it to be something that makes you smile. If you love it, that's your masterpiece! The key is to create a home you adore.

Step 4: Seek trusted, favorite resources for design and organizational inspiration. Flip back to page 185 for links to all my go-to design favorites.

ACTION STEP

Make notes in your journal from the ideas you saw in your online resources. Treat this like a research paper or business presentation. Bring your best problem-solving skills to your own home!

WARNING: OBSTACLE AHEAD!

Use technology carefully to support your minimalist journey. Instagram can be helpful, but it can also be distracting. Please avoid the "shop the look" options! I once had a client tell me she had "champagne taste on a beer budget." While I found it amusing, I realized that many people might feel that same way. Instead of thinking in terms of spending money, reframe that feeling and begin to think in terms of what resources you already own. Think, "How can I use the items already in my home wisely to get the champagne look without price-tag regret?"

As much as you can, focus on owning your interior design style rather than comparing your home to what someone else's home looks like. Don't compare yourself to your friends, family, or design bloggers. This is your space to create and grow, and your household needs your unique touch. Use online tools for inspiration, not replication.

Step 5. Tell your space to "speak clearly." If these walls could speak, what would they say? Your choice of design speaks to what you're trying to communicate. What does it say to you? To those you love? Make sure it's saying what you want it to express.

Questions to Ask

When it comes to redesigning your space, it's important to pause and think through the following questions:

- What kind of learner am I? Visual, auditory, or kinesthetic? This impacts how you will design the space.
- Am I concerned with how the space feels?
- Are textures important to me?
- What are my favorite scents and in what spaces do they belong? For the entryway, do I want it to smell like bread dough, herbs, or citrus? Scents are part of the experience! (For example, peppermint essential oil is my favorite to freshen our bath area.)
- Do I need visually clear spaces?
- What words do I want to use to describe my home?

Picture Your Ideal Room/Space

Now that you've considered the kind of space that will work for you, let's jot it all down.

Journal Activity

Write a journal entry describing your ideal home. It may look something like this:

When people walk into my home, I want them to feel a rush of relief, the warmth of pine plus the aroma of fresh bread baking in the oven. I want them to see well-worn fabrics; natural items with textures like stone, metal, and glass; cotton curtains; and bright light streaming in. I want clean lines but a cozy and imperfect feel. I want them to have a place to put their shoes, hang their coat or keys, and sit for a cup of tea to relax. I use these words to describe my home: safe, haven, relaxing, grace-filled, sacred, peace-filled, playful, positive energy.

Find elements that are similar to what you're looking for on Pinterest and Instagram. Try using helpful search terms such as "small bath solutions" or "narrow entryway." Bookmark and pin the pictures that give you one or more solid solutions. Avoid over-cluttering your Pinterest space!

ACTION STEP:

Create a Pinterest Board for each area. You're welcome to follow me on Pinterest as well and snoop my boards (see page 185).

For your entryway, closets, and bathroom, it's time to ask: What needs to occupy the space? Does your entryway need 17 different organizers when 2 would do? What would you do if you sold expensive items out of the space?

Let's pause and chat about money when it comes to design. Avoid the comparison trap of wishing for someone else's numbers. If you catch yourself spending time thinking of what other people have, reframe that mind-set and think of what you're grateful for that you do have. To help you with this, write a gratitude list in your journal. When you look at your budget, take a deep breath and think of what you're thankful for. And no matter what the numbers look like, you can always say, "I'm grateful for a new start!"

In addition to choosing gratitude, you can choose to use inexpensive solutions. One of my clients decided to remove the door of the coat closet because it was turned the wrong way for the flow of foot traffic. Another client repurposed a shelving unit and assigned each family member a set location for shoes. She grabbed a bench from another room for the girls to sit on while putting on shoes, and as a result, her entire mornings were transformed. The kids didn't fight while trying to get ready.

▶ None of these changes cost money; they simply utilize resources you already have. Consider your current organizational problems and come up with creative solutions to make your spaces functional and well designed.

Think of this redecorating of your entry, closets, and main bath as your first go at minimalism. Once you've decluttered the rest of your home, you may find that you want this space to have a different function or aesthetic. For now, be comfortable with this rough draft!

New Uses for New Spaces

Now that you've been able to clear out the excess in a few areas, you may have more open space than you're used to. If you feel grief or anxiety when you look around, refer back to the Feelings Checklist on page 27 before reading on.

You have a few options with regard to your new space. Open space can actually be its own design element—not every space needs to be filled. You can also consider other overcrowded systems in your house and shift some categories over to utilize this newfound space. If you plan on doing this, proceed with caution! The last thing you want to do is get discouraged by having your new clear spaces merely hijacked by chaos from other areas. I recommend living with a space when you first open it up. Leave it open for five to seven days. See how the space feels to you. Think through possible storage solutions for the space.

Minimalist Concept
Be bold and wait. Answers will take time to unfold.

Here are some ideas for creative storage:

There is no box. Don't just think outside the box; think as if there isn't a box at all! It's important to have complete freedom when thinking of how to design this space. Store pantry items in the bedroom closet? Sure! Put a desk in the kitchen as extra food prep space? I did. Totally acceptable, as long as you're at peace with it. Move and switch and change to your heart's content.

Rearrange furniture. To maximize efficiency while minimizing items, consider rearranging furniture. Sometimes, a small change can open up surprising additional space. Before you do, it's helpful to measure and use blue painter's tape to mark where you'd like different pieces to go.

Separate sets or modify furniture. I donated my piano and kept the bench. I put mittens inside the piano bench and used it to create an entryway spot for my kids' shoes. Need to repurpose a chair? Take the legs off to lower it and make it child size. I recently did this in my daughter's room so her chinchilla wouldn't hide under the chair while it roamed her room. Try not to have excess furniture. How do your furniture pieces relate or "talk" to each other? Do they work well with other pieces? Watch for sharp corners, narrow pathways that can get clogged, and trip hazards. Think in terms of balance, symmetry, and less is more. I often recommend looking online and in retail stores to see how furniture is staged for a pleasing look.

Storage can be inside a cupboard, basket, or underneath furniture such as benches. Look for items with components that can be used in multiple ways. Take off lids, put lids on, disguise it as something else, paint it, break off an extra piece (I did this to a clock), and use it in a new way.

DESIGN TIP:

If your room lacks natural light, add elements that enhance light, such as mirrors near light fixtures.

Style & Design

As you learn about minimalism, you'll find that there are strong variances between different kinds of minimalist aesthetics, such as more traditional and mid-century modern. You might also see the influence of Japanese minimalism (low furniture and natural material floor coverings), which I'm particularly fond of due to my Japanese side of the family. Another cultural influence upon minimalism is the Scandinavian style, in which white walls and furniture, simply designed, characterize spaces. Learn about these if this concept interests you. What cultural design aesthetics speak to you?

In the bathroom, make sure you have enough space for the people in your home to go about their daily routines. Reuse glass jars as decorative ways to store, label, and display everyday items. I use small glass jars for my homemade zero-waste toothpaste. But be careful! I forgot to label it, and my husband confused it with the homemade deodorant. The look on his face was priceless when he brushed his teeth with deodorant!

In the entryway, add a mirror or shaker hooks for space-saving organization that is visually appealing. Consider the shapes of your space. If you have square windows, consider a contrasting circular mirror.

We'll apply the same principles to decorative items as we did to furniture. Ask yourself these questions:

- Does this item make a major statement in my home?
- Is this a "masterpiece" (in my eyes) worthy of display?
- Does this item play well with other items in this space?
- Does this space need a fresh coat of paint?

Oftentimes, a lighter paint color is needed. Talk to a professional painter or a specialty paint store owner for your unique needs if your walls are plaster, as painting plaster is different from painting drywall. You can also use any leftover paint to paint decorative items.

Remember to reward yourself for your newly redesigned space. You don't need to wait for it to be perfect before you celebrate—it can take time to complete your vision! Reward yourself with a visit with your best friend, a party with 30 of your closest family members, or just a warm cup of tea alone—just take time to celebrate and take a deep breath, because we're going to keep going! Next, we'll head over to your home office area.

THREE

The Home Office

"You can't go back and
change the beginning,
but you can start where
you are and change
the ending."

—UNKNOWN

My home office was an area where I especially struggled in my decluttering journey. Old notes, financial documents, desk clutter, mail, school papers, and even digital clutter created a monumental mess. Clearing this space also brought up issues from the past and strong emotions. I knew I needed a fresh start to create a new, better ending to the mess in my office and finances!

Where to Start?

With the rise of our mobile side gig economy, the concept of the home office has grown and changed quickly over the last few decades. Whether you work from home or manage a busy household, almost everyone has a place they use for managing paperwork. This space has specific challenges. Once you clear out and simplify this space, you can be more productive. You might even end up having some extra space in there to create a meditation or exercise area to increase mind-body productivity! In this chapter, we'll tackle these areas:

- Home office
- Desk
- Study area
- Family calendar area
- Mail center

Every successful household needs a home office command center. You might not have the square footage for a dedicated room, but with a bit of creativity, a corner nook can work just as well. No matter how big or small your home office, order and simplicity are your best assets.

If you share a space with a partner, you'll want to separate their belongings from yours. When my husband first left his job to work from home, we shared the same desk and the same computer. Let's just say it led to conflict—our work styles are completely different. I am a detail- and task-oriented person, and he's more of a visionary. He likes piles of paper on the floor; I prefer everything clean, put away, and easy to find. And I didn't want merely the appearance of clean spaces, only to have disastrous desk drawers hiding clutter. We had to find a way to create our office space in a way that made sense to both of us. We tried a dozen different configurations before we found what worked for us. Don't despair if your space needs to be redesigned in the future or if your co-sharing space doesn't work for you right now. Take some deep breaths and try to imagine what will work while you're sorting papers. Let your partner sort papers in his or her own realm.

We'll get to more solutions in the Reimagining Your Space section (page 52). Just know that overcoming challenges can be an incredible bonding and team-building experience for you and your partner. For now, let's dive into simple strategies to save you time and money in your office space.

Sorting & Logistics

Let's start by declaring a consistent "office day" each week. I adopted this concept when I was first decluttering. My addiction to paper had grown to a serious issue bigger than just a once-a-week declutter. I had left my corporate job in the insurance industry where every piece of paper was precious, and I had to learn a new set of priorities for running a home office. Whether you're a business owner or a stay-at-home parent or both, you don't need to save every piece of paper. I like the concept of a weekly office day on a maintenance level, but most households will need to do both a daily office routine and a weekly office day. Like in chapter 1, home office decluttering is achieved through both Simplicity Self-Care Dates (page 12) and several Quantum Sprints (page 12).

Step 1: The First Pass
Timer Set: 15 minutes

Materials Needed

1 black trash bag for trash

1 shredding bin

1 tub or black trash bag for donating

1 to 4 plastic Delivery Tubs for other locations in your home

Decluttering Journal and pen

Black marker

File folders

Decluttering Chart (page 173)

Phone for "before" photos

1. Take a "before" photo or two.

2. Decide what to keep and what to discard. Place current bills into one folder and mark the tab BILLS with the black marker. Identify and keep tax records in a separate file, cabinet, or file box.

3. Toss junk mail, unread advertisements, and magazines into the recycling bag. Even if you think there might be something useful in there, resist the urge to open it. Stay focused and move quickly so you don't get stuck reading through old notes or mail like I used to!

4. Toss any items that contain sensitive information into the shredding bin.

5. Place everything else in an empty file folder or more than one as needed. We'll get to that file in the next step.

As you go through papers, you may think of tasks that need to be done. Do you need to file forms at your local tax office? Did you locate a receipt for an item to return? Write these thoughts in your journal so you can schedule and accomplish those tasks after you're done with this quick first step.

SUSTAINABILITY TIP:

Most communities have a free shredding day where you can take papers with sensitive information to be shredded and recycled. If it's a year away, ask friends for a shredder to borrow. You can use the shredding, depending on composition, to compost your garden for a sustainable win.

ACTION STEP:

Each time you enter your home office space, do tasks in the same order. For example, check your priority list and work on your most urgent, time-sensitive task first. Allocate a specific time for non-urgent tasks, filing, and checking e-mail.

Step 2: The Big Sort

Timer Set: 30 to 50 minutes with multiple sessions as needed

Materials Needed

1 black trash bag for trash

1 tub or black trash bag for donating

1 plastic tub for items to sell

Tracking Sheet for Items to Sell (page 178)

1 plastic tub for items to be given away to specific people

1 to 4 plastic Delivery Tubs for other locations in your home

Decluttering Journal and pen

Uplifting music or podcast

Labeling supplies

Decluttering Chart (page 173)

Recycling Tub

Shredding bin

Scissors for cutting up old credit cards, gift cards, promo cards, etc.

Black marker for writing on file folders

Extra 3-ring binders (my favorite are stainless-steel indestructible binders from the medical or automotive industry available on eBay—they're more expensive than their plastic counterparts but last forever)

Heavy-duty 3-ring hole punch

Heavy-duty trash bags

Filing cabinet or file box

Additional hanging files (I recommend the kind that don't have plastic tabs but instead have a tab that is part of the file itself—this little hack has saved me hours of frustration when the tabs would get loose and fall off)

Fire-safe box (it's worth it)

Water bottle and snack

1. As you go, place any items or papers that don't belong in the home office in the Delivery Tub. Leave enough time at the end of each session to deliver papers or items to the general location where they should be in the house.

2. Now that you have the papers together that should stay in the office, you'll want to sort them into categories. You can write out a rough draft of your categories in your Decluttering Journal. As you sort, you can always change the categories. Here's an example:

   Bills to pay: It's helpful to also add an annual calendar chart that lists your annual or biannual bills so you can watch for upcoming expenditures (see page 176).

   Passwords/login: It's vital to keep a paper log of your passwords. Unfortunately, I know the importance of this with the sudden death of loved ones. Put this document in your firebox and make a note on the calendar to update it once per quarter or whenever you change a password.

   Vital papers: Documents such as birth certificates, real estate deeds, rental leases, social security cards, marriage licenses, vehicle titles, wills, and estate papers will also go in your firebox. Please, for your loved ones, go put these items in the box right now.

Vehicle repair receipts: It's helpful to be able to track your vehicle's maintenance or use these for resale purposes.

Household maintenance: This might include names of paints, warranties, or manuals for items like the hot water heater, furnace, or AC. Don't keep documentation from faucets or small gadgets. Keeping digital manuals and warranties is fine.

Household appliances: Keep the manuals and warranties for your washer, dryer, fridge, dishwasher, garbage disposal, and microwave.

Retirement investments: This includes any life insurance, pension, or social security–related documents.

Current projects: This is where you keep action items, such as papers that need to be signed for school, paperwork for the gas company that needs a new signature, and other items that need attending to but aren't bills.

Place these papers in your hanging files and file them in the cabinet or file box in order of use with "bills to pay" first.

ACTION STEP:

Name your digital and physical files with the same titles. Use the first words that come to mind when naming your files. Keep your sanity and organize consistently. Google Drive is my go-to for digital online storage. For business receipts, I prefer Neat.com.

As with the previous decluttering, don't worry if this takes a significant amount of time. You may need several sessions in order to achieve the type of organization and clarity you desire for your home office. After all, you didn't collect all this paperwork in one day!

For items that need to be sold, add a short description to the Tracking Sheet for Items to Sell (page 178). This sheet will help you track where you've listed the ad to sell the item, how much you've offered the item for, and how much you ended up selling it for.

Step 3: Deliver/Sell/Donate

Deliver items where they belong just like you did in chapter 1 (page 20). All green smoothie cups need to go back to the kitchen (I have one on my desk right now). Books go back to the bookshelf in the living room; don't worry if that needs decluttering, too. I like to ask my children to help deliver items. It teaches them to declutter and keep items in the correct space. If you have teens, you can put them in charge of selling items and provide them with a small "commission" as a way to teach them financial literacy. Donate any unused folders to your local school or charity. Consider here if you want to keep or downsize furniture, including filing cabinets, desks, bookshelves, or extra chairs. Once you've sorted the paper clutter, you might find your needs have changed and you're ready to sell unnecessary furniture.

I found there was less to sell here in the office than in other areas of the home, with the exception of old electronics. You can add unused electronics to the Tracking Sheet for Items to Sell (page 178). Try not to allow unused devices to remain past their useful life span, and recycle the boxes they came in as well.

When you think about what kind of storage works best for this area, shop your house first and look for multiuse items. Get creative and keep an eye on that recycling bin for possible solutions for creative storage containers to categorize papers if you don't own a filing cabinet. I had a client use empty cereal boxes cut up and covered with professional-looking contact paper for her filing system.

MONEY-SAVING TIP:

If you need a filing cabinet, check Facebook Marketplace or local auction advertisements. You can often find free or low-cost cabinets being sold by businesses when they upgrade and need to eliminate older cabinets. A cheap can of paint is often all that is needed to update a sturdy cabinet's exterior.

Step 4: Tracking and Celebrating

If you are tracking on your Decluttering Chart (page 173), update it now. This chart is a simple grid with 500 small squares. When you donate an item, you can place an X in one square. You're in charge of how to mark off the boxes on the chart; you can do one X per item or per box. Set a reward at the end of the sheet or at the number of X's that represents your goal. Celebrate each accomplishment as you bring order to your office space.

Minimalist Concept
Tracking is the key to get you where you want to be.

Saying Goodbye to Stuff

Planners, notebooks, stationery, and any type of office supply make me giddy. When I adopted the minimalism lifestyle, I realized I didn't need all this extra stuff in my home office to run a successful household or business. My log home has 1,400 square feet, and in it, I run multiple businesses and homeschool my six children—I can't afford to have too much of anything extra in my office space!

Here is a suggested list of items to be donated or discarded:

- Old mismatched file folders that don't fit your filing cabinet
- Wrinkled plastic page protectors. You won't ever straighten them out enough to use.
- Extra or out-of-date calendars half written in
- Electronic chargers that don't go to any devices still in the house
- Old informational CDs/DVDs that are out-of-date
- Tacks when you don't have a bulletin board anymore
- Extra or nonworking pens

How much is too much? Do you need 500 pens? My dad laughs at me because that's totally him. He is a maximalist when it comes to pens and random flashlights in his office. I argue that if I have one pen and one flashlight to write and to see, I keep much better track of it all. The reality is most of the time you'll need something in the middle of those two extremes. Choose an amount that works for you and test it out for a week. If it doesn't work, change it.

One of the biggest hang-ups that my clients have with paperwork is the valid question: "What if I need that?" The main items you'll need to keep are tax documents, bank statements, and anything legal, which is hopefully already in your firebox. Beyond that, in our digital age, you don't need to keep most of your monthly bills. If ever you need an item, you can contact the company involved and ask.

You'll want to prepare yourself for some emotions that may come up when decluttering your papers. Let's check out the following Feelings Checklist.

Feelings Checklist

You may find, like I did, that this home office space is hard on the emotions. This is not because you're emotionally attached to paper per se; it's all that the paper represents. Time. Money. Decisions. Relationships. Everything about your home meets here.

Journal through your Feelings Checklist here, making a list of what you feel as you declutter this room. Pay close attention to repeating thoughts. Add a sentence of explanation to each of the feelings in your list. This will help you identify exactly what you are experiencing:

- **Fear:** What if I need that paper?
- **Overwhelm:** Will this ever end?
- **Relief:** It feels good to finally tackle this!
- **Shame:** We're totally broke, and now I have to see it in black-and-white on all these bills.
- **Excitement:** At last, I'm finally able to find the papers/passwords/documents when I need them.
- **Healing:** What a load off. I have put that behind me.
- **Clarity:** I feel so together now. ▶

▶ • **Unnamed pain:** I've had multiple clients experience strong psychological and even physical responses of pain decluttering this area. If this is you, please seek additional help. Emotional healing is possible but takes time. Journal about what it would look like to have your home office be a healing space for you.

WARNING: OBSTACLE AHEAD!

Pain seeks pleasure. Avoid reactive spending or revenge spending if you are the "saving" type of personality in your home. Resist the urge to run from the panic in this area of your home. I get it—I've been completely broke (and broken!) multiple times in our financial journey. I didn't want to sit at my desk or open my checkbook. I would want to spend money that we didn't have, just to prove to myself that we weren't poor. There's no judgment from me if you've spent money when you knew you shouldn't have. The important thing is for you to make a new choice going forward.

Reimagining Your Space

Now begins the fun part of decluttering: the redesigning! First, evaluate the location of your home office. My office has changed several times, from the kitchen nook to front and center in our living room.

We have an extra-large bedroom that we partitioned in half to make better use of the space as an office. Walk through your home with new eyes, and think about what will help you work best. Do you need to be near the family in order to give instructions for dinner prep, or do you need complete quiet to make important phone calls? This can help you determine where you set up shop.

Picture Your Perfect Room

When you close your eyes, what do you want to see in a home office? What inspires you? Do you need different books, files, or supplies to accomplish your tasks? Start with your personal preferences. Do you want everything placed conveniently out of sight? It all begins with envisioning what works for you.

MONEY-SAVING TIP:

Budget ahead for office supplies. Take advantage of tax abatement or tax-free days prior to the start of a new school year to stock up on basic supplies, such as paper and pencils. Only buy what you know you will use in a 12-month span. Always err on the side of fewer supplies.

I adore decorating with books, but my minimalist side uses books from our local library. I borrow books that inspire me as I research a particular topic. When I choose a new topic, I switch out the books and borrow new ones. Library book decor is my go-to for sprucing up an office space with zero waste as an added benefit.

New Uses for New Spaces

As you declutter and categorize your home office, you may consider downsizing your furniture. When you've simplified your paper collection, you may find new possibilities open up in terms of how your space is used. In the four-step process of decluttering, did you downsize your filing cabinet from a four-drawer to a two-drawer like I did? Did you decide that you work just as well at a small desk as a larger desk? Now that you've opened up additional square footage, consider new uses for your space. Do you have room now for a yoga mat? What about a few new plants? Enjoy adding new tasks to the space cautiously. I tended to overwork my space by adding too many activities to a small area. Go slowly and think through what will work best for your new decluttered space.

Style and Design

As you look to style your home office, consider how to display everyday items in a new way. Carefully curate this, as it can easily look cluttered or tacky. Keep consistent color schemes. I recommend using 80 percent of your base color in decor, 15 percent in a primary accent color, and 5 percent in a secondary accent color. This could include main furniture like a desk or small accent pieces like lamps or even pencils. Look at each item's color and shape and see how it interacts with the space you have.

Your desks and chairs don't need to be fancy; in fact, simple lines are more versatile and visually pleasing. Choose timeless looks that can be updated with minor changes like new hardware or accessories. If you must buy a desk, look for a used one first. I found my previously owned dream desk for a ridiculously low price. As a nice bonus, it lowered the demand for new items to be manufactured.

Consider wall art and any need for chalkboards or whiteboards. Can you use those as part of your design? You can use chalkboards for tracking household or business items, with a matching one for inspirational quotes. Look for beautiful items that you can use in a practical way.

Choose one item that inspires you to reach your next goal, whatever that may be, and keep it on your desk. A single seashell currently sits on my desk for a reminder of an upcoming trip to the coast. What are you working toward? This will provide you with a visual reminder to encourage you daily and help you face obstacles when hard days come.

Remember to clear your desk each evening. I call it "closing up shop." This routine will ensure that you keep your mind and desk ready and prepared for the next day.

Now that you've decluttered your entryway, closets, bath, and home office, you have a significant percentage of your daily spaces conquered. Maintaining clean and open spaces is easier when these areas are under control. As a reminder, always be on the lookout for patterns of impeded flow and bottlenecks. Of course, life happens, so if you have a medical emergency, busy season of travel, or the arrival of a new baby, don't stress! Now that you've started the process, it's much easier to pick up these practices again and turn them into habits.

Congrats on all the amazing progress you've made to this point! Next up are the kids' rooms and/or playroom. With six wild and beautiful children running around my little log home, I'm excited to share my strategies for sanity with you in these precious spaces.

FOUR

Kids' Bedrooms and Playrooms

"Children are not a burden
to escape or endure; they are
a blessing that drive us."

—KIM BRENNEMAN

I could write an entire book solely on decluttering kids' rooms, but as this is a minimalist book, let's keep the discussion straightforward and simple! You'll apply the same process here that you've used in previous rooms.

My six children range in age from toddler to young adult, but your family composition might look different. I'll be using the following terms to classify the different age ranges whenever applicable:

Young child: newborn to age 5

Elementary-age child: 6 to 12 years old

Young adult: 13 years old to college age

When I first started decluttering my kids' rooms, I realized that if I was upset with the volume of toys scattered everywhere, I also needed to control the number of items they had. My children needed a system, and it was completely unreasonable for me to expect them to put their items away when there was too much to put away!

Where to Start?

Rome wasn't built in a day. Kids' rooms aren't decluttered in a day. You'll need a plan, so grab your journal and let's get started!

Journal Activity

Start by writing down a list of everything that frustrates you about the kids' space. Your list might look like mine did:

- Clothes all over the floor
- Toys everywhere
- Can't walk through safely

- Food stains
- Piles of school papers
- Can't find anything, including the bed
- The smell

Next, write a list of how your kids feel about their space. Ask them these questions over a peaceful dinner or when they're snuggled on the couch in the evening. Always start with the positive:

- What is your favorite spot in the house?
- What do you like best about your bedroom/playroom?
- What's your favorite activity in that room?
- Do you think you have enough space to do that?
- What would you change if you could about your room?
- Is there anything fun that you'd like to add to that room? Be prepared for fun answers like "indoor swimming pool," "two-story slide," and "giraffe"—my kids actually suggested these.

Minimalist Concept
I am responsible for the items that come into and stay in my home.

If you have a partner, take some time to journal about how this person is involved with the clutter in the kids' bedrooms or playrooms. Making a short list of the other caretaker's involvement will provide important insight. Does your partner add to the mess, clean it, or ignore it completely? List ways that your partner can help and support your efforts. This journal entry will be valuable to review before discussing the children's rooms with your partner.

Sorting and Logistics

New habits take time to create, and it will take time to bring others—especially children—on board with your vision. Let's break down this strategy into the four manageable steps we've used in previous rooms.

Step 1: The First Pass
Timer Set: 15 minutes

Materials Needed

1 garbage bag for trash

1 garbage bag for donations

1 Delivery Tub

Decluttering Journal and pen

Decluttering Chart (page 173)

Be prepared for *anything* you may find in your children's rooms. Take your "before" picture now, not to shame your children but to encourage them at the end of the decluttering process when the "after" photo shows progress. Children don't have the cognitive framework to organize physical items like we do and shouldn't be shamed for that lack of skill. My four-year-old currently has an emotional attachment to a metal bolt with two washers. In my mind it's not important, but it means the world to him. My children also love to build piles. My children like to save sticky ice pop sticks as sentimental items and pile important papers on top, so I always remind myself to be patient with what I find tucked away.

In addition to children's sentimental items, you may also find old outgrown clothing, school papers or projects, crafts, art supplies, shoes, winter coats, toys, board games, video or tech accessories, bedsheets, towels, miscellaneous linens, and 16 million mismatched socks. Try to think of what your child needs to accomplish in this space as you go through the first pass of tidying, and evaluate what items are necessary. Leave time at the end of this step to deliver the items in your Delivery Tub and fill out the squares in your Decluttering Chart (page 173). If you don't have time to deliver the items, do enough to close the lid and return to it in step 2. Keep the Delivery Tub in your Decluttering Command Station until your next step.

Journal Activity

Take a moment to look around the child's room from a child's perspective. What does your child do in this space? Your list might look like this:

Young child: sleep, play unattended safely, look at books, draw with crayons and washable markers, read board books

Elementary-age child: do homework, make art projects, play pretend, listen to music, do science experiments, read, talk on the phone, and play video games with friends

Young adult: sleep, do homework, play, get dressed, read, hang out with friends, play computer games, do hair and makeup, keep sentimental items, watch movies, store books and school supplies

Now that you've written down in your Decluttering Journal what tasks your child does in this room, ask yourself, "Am I happy with how this room is working?" Answer this question in your journal with detail, noting both what's working well and what isn't.

Some things are likely working well in your kids' spaces; for instance, your children are going to bed, in their bed, on time each night. Some things may not be working as well—maybe they refuse to do their homework peacefully in this space. Once you've charted this out in your journal, you can begin to identify why this space isn't working. Focus your efforts on the spot that is a priority to you in this quick first pass.

Your child especially needs to know that you are 100,000,000 percent in their corner. If you have had conflicts in the past around cleaning, you may need to rebuild that bridge of trust now. Use words and actions. Show your child daily that you are committed to setting them up for success.

Here are some supportive phrases you can use:

"Is there anything else that you need?"
"How can I help you right now?"
"I'm always thinking about you."

Watch your tone carefully to avoid any hint of sarcasm, as some children are sensitive to tone even if you're being completely sincere. The aim is to build trust.

The other side of earning and maintaining trust is setting consistent, healthy boundaries of personal responsibility. Allowing children to be active participants in the decluttering process is as important as the decluttering itself. In the first pass, you can enlist the residents of that particular room. Invite them to do a quick sort with you. I would not use music or media of any kind during this sort with your child. This is a relationship-building time between you and your child. Keep expectations low and give your child ample praise for participating in any way.

WARNING: OBSTACLE AHEAD!

If you or your child has struggled with anger in the past, tread lightly. Write a list of what triggers your anger and your child's anger in your journal. Take a minute to write down what has caused anger in the past, noting causes, time of day, and circumstances as well. It might help to make sure you've got a rested, relaxed, and well-fed young participant going into this.

The goal of this first pass is for team-building and identifying a few opportunities and frustration points. You want to get rid of trash and random unused items. Identify a few things to donate and deliver misplaced items to the correct rooms of the house. Help your child see their room in a whole new way, as a realm of their own responsibility, for their benefit. If your child is old enough, talk through your vision of what the room can be as you do this first pass together.

Allow enough time for quick deliveries at the end of this first step. If your child is helping, you can set a timer and race each other to deliver items to other rooms of the house. You'll want to start the next step with a mostly empty Delivery Tub.

WARNING: OBSTACLE AHEAD!

When decluttering a child's room, special considerations should always be taken for children with autism or who experience issues with sensory overload. You may even include your child's counselor, teacher, or other parent in your plan prior to setting action steps in motion. Seeing the room from your child's perspective is especially important for these children, as is using extra wisdom and grace.

Getting Kids On Board

When you're preparing to make changes in a child's space, getting them to understand and appreciate the idea of simplifying their space is an important first step, especially when it means getting rid of things they own. Here are some ways to encourage them:

Let them watch you. You are the example. Let them see you simplifying your areas before you touch theirs. Make sure they see what you are donating and explain why. And allow them to join in the celebration of completion.

Explain why giving is good. You can tell them, "We're going to be sharing some of the items that are extra for us with others who may not have enough. Then we will have a cleaner house with more room to play!"

Make it fun and reward them. You can say, "We want to have more time to make ice cream rather than always being stuck cleaning—doesn't that sound good? Let's tidy up together and then make ice cream." I have done this, and then I make homemade ice cream as a reward!

Step 2: The Big Sort

Timer Set: 15 to 90 minutes per session (depending on age and ability) with multiple sessions

Materials Needed

1 black trash bag for trash

1 black trash bag for donating

1 plastic Delivery Tub

1 plastic Sell Tub

1 plastic tub for items to be given away to specific people (such as items that kids want to share)

Decluttering Journal and pen

Decluttering Chart (page 173)

Uplifting music that your child enjoys if they are helping you

Labeling supplies

Water bottle(s) and snack to share if your child is helping

The time frame for this should be flexible based on the age and needs of your child. Take careful note of frustration levels (of both you and your child). Avoid angry cleaning—the more fun you can have doing it, the easier it will be. Give your child age-appropriate jobs:

- A young child can help place items in the correct sorting bins.
- An elementary-age child can help label the bins of toys and sort small pieces.
- A young adult child can carry heavy items for donation to the vehicle.

Children need help creating categories. You'll even want to guide and support young adult children, as each person may understand "organization" differently. Ask open-ended questions about what categories make sense to them, like "How do you think we should organize your craft supplies?" You may want to enlist the child's help to deliver items from your Delivery Tub while you create the categories for them inside the room. Set aside time for delivering items with each decluttering session.

Part of the process of decluttering is learning to work together. How do you and your child see the categories? Are they a visual learner? Are they tactile with a love of textures? Do they need to move constantly? Play to your child's strengths and also to yours. Do you need more organization than they do? Perhaps you want more color in the playroom? Many parents know to focus on their child, but the kids' rooms must also work for the parents. Cooperation and compromise are key here, and finding solutions is an ongoing process.

When doing a big sort in a playroom, I recommend setting up a toy library system. Some local libraries have one, which is a fantastic resource to utilize, and I recommend it for your home toys as well. Many children enjoy the thrill of checking out something from the "library," especially elementary-age children.

Setting Up a Toy Library

Keep out a few small favorite toys, stuffed animals, dolls, or cars that children will have unlimited access to. Store these in a special box and provide each child with one unique box.

Then sort the rest of the toys and activities by categories. You can even subcategorize per child if you have a wide age gap and a wide variation of age-appropriate toys.

Our toy library looks like this:

1. Dolls and clothing accessories

2. Origami—paper, instruction books, and current projects

3. Stuffed animals

4. Costumes

5. Mechanical building sets

6. Board games

7. Wooden blocks

8. Math-U-See counting blocks

9. Seashells and fossils

10. Noah's Ark with wooden animals

11. Puzzles

The rules of the library are simple. A child can check out one container at a time with permission. Once the activity is done, the container must be completely put away before they can "check out" another one. Make this a strict rule! Since I have six kids who may be in different locations, I allow two checked-out containers at any given time—do whatever works for you. You may choose to locate the toy library on high shelves or in a locked cabinet.

Minimalist Concept
*If you make a mess,
you clean it up.*

Now is when you'll start conversations with your child about what to keep and what to share. I like to use the word "share" rather than the phrase "get rid of." Many children naturally gravitate toward relating to other people, and sharing is a more positive way of framing the release of items from their possession. Teaching them to share is an ongoing challenge and a lifelong skill, and you can help them see the good in sharing what they have with others.

By now your children have seen you declutter the entryway, the communal closets, the bathroom, and your home office area. Those changes may have taken place over several weeks or several months. Hopefully, they've seen the benefits, now that they have an easier time finding their shoes in the entryway. Even so, be prepared for the fact that your child may not be emotionally ready to release anything. The main skill that you're teaching is sorting at this step. Be patient. Model generosity; let them see you donate your own items in other rooms. Build trust and routines as you sort.

Step 3: Deliver/Sell/Donate

Send young children out on simple deliveries. Make it a game or a race. Toddlers can take their socks to a sock box located by the shoes. Elementary-age children can take papers to the recycling bin. Young adult children can take the donation bag to the vehicle (most of the time without getting anything out of the donation bag to sneak back into the house). Choose tasks that are child- and age-appropriate, and shower them with praise and gratitude for even small tasks completed.

Part of the purpose of involving your children in this step is so you can create a home your children understand and can help operate. When they know where to deliver items, they can put things away themselves. When they see you recycling, they understand what items can be recycled and how to sort them. When they see you donate items, they understand the value of sharing.

Now, I had many setbacks in my decluttering journey where I didn't always feel like being generous, and my children had a front row seat to my failures. Allow your children to not be perfect in the process and give yourself grace as well. I know I sure needed grace in this journey! However, I talked my children through the intentional changes in my own life and explained why I made these changes—this communication led me to new ways of parenting.

As a parent, I learned to set a new example by:

- No longer hanging out with friends who always wanted to go shopping
- Making time for hiking and outdoor adventures for my children's playdates
- Having vital conversations with family members, allowing children to hear when appropriate
- Setting up a weekly donation pickup with a local charity
- Reading books and blogs, and watching YouTube videos on decluttering with my children
- Not going to garage sales every Friday and using the free time for more meaningful activities

You may also involve young adult children in giving them freedom to sell or donate anything they wish. This one was hard for me! Giving up control is precarious, especially if you have a particularly generous child. I had to allow my daughter to give away items that I didn't necessarily want her to. But it changed my own heart, increased my generosity, and gave her the confidence to trust herself to make a good decision.

Step 4: Tracking and Celebrating

Give your child their own Decluttering Chart (page 173) for items in their bedroom or playroom. Print out a 500-square spreadsheet and tape it to the back of their bedroom door. For elementary-age and young adult children, show them where the Decluttering Command Center is and give them permission to get their own donation garbage bag. Again, each child will need guidance depending on their age and ability. Set a reasonable goal. When you hit the decluttering goal, celebrate! Our celebrations included homemade ice cream for breakfast. While enjoying the special treat, we talked about how much easier it is to find their favorite toys and how much more time we have to make special treats like ice cream since we aren't cleaning all the time. See my own decluttering marketing tool there? Ice cream is a great motivator!

Another reward is to give them money from items that they sell. This was a strong motivator for one of my children, as he loves numbers and wanted to buy his own fish tank. I may have been a customer and "bought" toys to donate once or twice—this can be a smart way to get a resistant child to warm up to the concept!

You can also place a young adult child in charge of labeling and managing the toy library. That child can also be in charge of fixing, donating, or discarding toys with your direction. This teaches decision-making skills and personal responsibility as well as serving younger members of the household. It also delegates authority from you to the older child and allows for their development of leadership skills.

Saying Goodbye to Stuff

The benefits of creating a minimalist lifestyle are amplified when we model that lifestyle for our children as we say "goodbye to stuff."

Children benefit directly by seeing an example of how to:

- Choose to value other people more than stuff
- Work together toward a common goal
- Embrace new experiences
- Release emotional attachments to inanimate objects
- Savor memories by telling stories instead of holding on to a physical memento

Questions to Ask

Perhaps you and your child both have a strong attachment to certain items. Use the following questions to gain clarity for yourself and as a starting place for discussions with your child.

- How much will it cost to replace this item if I need it later?
- How much trouble would it be to find this item again in terms of time and effort?

- How much would it impact other family members in my house if I got rid of this item now?
- Do I have space to store this?
- Will this matter in 10 years?
- What conversations will I need to have with family members when I eliminate this item?

Affirmation Statements (for Kids)

People are more important than stuff.
We need to use what we have before we can have more.
We need to be good stewards of our world's resources.
We are happy to share with others.
We love to go on adventures!
We bring the fun!

One of my largest struggles was setting clear, firm boundaries with other family members about what I would allow in my home. Having those hard-but-healing conversations about boundaries and expectations will set you up for long-term peace in your decluttering journey. I wish I had initiated those conversations earlier in my journey. I waited two years to bring up the furniture temporarily "stored" in my living room. I did not always handle the issues of family gift-giving correctly either. I declined gifts in frustration and anger instead of with grace and kindness. I allowed over-gifting to steal the joy from the holidays several years in a row before I asked for "adventure" gifts, like a zoo membership or a science museum family pass. But over time, while communicating with family members, I was able to rid myself of my insecurities. The parenting confidence I gained started with open conversations with my family about how and why I was trying to raise children the minimalist way.

Teach your family to "ask first" before giving gifts to your children (and not in front of the children!). Many times, a simple explanation of "experience-oriented gifts" prior to holidays or birthdays can help families reduce the number of gifts given. Often, well-meaning family members simply need to know that a child would like art lessons or to go to horseback riding camp or to go out for ice cream. Other times, a firm stance of no gifts is the only option. Be free to make the best choice for your household. I recommend setting a clear, consistent standard; otherwise, over-gifting gets worse and escalates into power struggles.

One of my biggest challenges in cleaning out my children's bedrooms and the playroom was getting over my fear. I chose to let go of the fear of what others would say and no longer allow other people's gifts to determine what items I would keep in my home. With six children, gifts can quickly add up! I recommend moving the conversation away from a particular item or gift and more toward valuing the person as a gift-giver; the conversations will go much better.

Gift-giving can be a sweet expression of love within a family without being solely based on the transfer of material items. The alternatives may take time and multiple conversations, but a mutually agreeable solution is worth working toward.

Own Less, Live More

Here are some ways that children benefit from owning less and living more:

- General appreciation and gratitude
- Increased prioritization skills
- Sense of patterns and categories
- Better ability to focus on tactile tasks as they learn to sort
- A greater understanding of evaluating and naming feelings
- Environmental awareness through discussions of stewardship

Be sure to include your children in planning the deadline and rewards for when you complete each room-by-room transformation. Maintaining a simple home takes diligence, but having an end date in sight and talking through the benefits will help your children see the connection between the work and the rewards.

Attachment and Sentiment

Working through emotions and attachments can be a healing and growing exercise for both parents and children as they work together to declutter.

Feelings Checklist

It's important to journal your feelings as well as your child's. Some of the feelings that may come up for you both are:

- **Nostalgia**
- **Frustration**
- **Adoration** from bonding
- **Anxiety** about the future
- **Insecurity** in decision-making
- **Hopelessness** in dealing with those who don't support your efforts
- **Nervousness** about discussions with family members
- **Hope** for a peaceful childhood and a peaceful home
- **Clarity**
- **Excitement**

Either a strong positive or negative emotion can provide insight into areas of emotional healing. Which areas are healed? Which still need healing? Write what you're feeling or chronicle your child's emotions or voiced sentiments during decluttering.

A simple home doesn't solve hurting emotions, but it does make the space needed to address them in a healthy way.

Reimagining Your Space

Remember your childhood power of imagination? Harness that imagination here as you plan ways to redecorate and refresh your newly decluttered kids' spaces.

Picture Your (and Their) Perfect Room

Close your eyes and imagine the space. In your mind, clear out all the furniture and think of what you would put in its place. This exercise in imagination and visualization is incredibly useful as you redesign the space. I recommend you do this before you check online resources. This is your unique space, and your own imagination may yield even more innovative ideas than the Internet. I like to use my imagination for what the room could be even before I clear it. (You can choose to physically clear out everything, too, but I know my furniture-moving causes huge disruptions to my household, so I try to only move the furniture when I'm sure where it will go).

While you're picturing your new space, consider the ages and stages of your children. Look ahead five years. What kinds of changes are coming? With one girl and five boys from toddlers to teens, there's always something new happening in my house! Choose your decor, linens, and furniture with this in mind. Think in terms of color blocks, and try to use patterns strategically. I chose to use bed linens that were durable and white so I could easily sun-bleach them or replace them without trying too hard to match replacements as the boys grew.

Invite your child to imagine new layouts or design elements in their spaces. Even the youngest children have wonderfully creative ideas that are worthy of consideration. I've enjoyed including my children in designing their spaces and taken notes of how we could implement their ideas.

SUSTAINABILITY TIP:

Search eBay for natural fabrics for your children's room. Cotton sheets, blankets, or goose down comforters for colder climates are reusable for multiple children. You can often find brand-new linens with minor sewing asymmetry sold "as is" for much less than retail.

New Uses for New Spaces

Let's name the spaces in this room. Here's what works for us:

- Study space
- Project space
- Clothing space (capsule wardrobe, page 179)
- Free play space
- Sleep space

STUDY SPACE

You may need to think creatively about where to locate a study space. This will depend on the age of your child and their particular needs, but most children need a place that is both accessible and quiet. My elementary-age children work at wooden trays while sitting on the couch. My teens need their own desks. We are constantly reevaluating how study areas work best as the children grow. Whatever you choose, make it easy for your child to enjoy this space. Add a comfy chair, a pillow, a plant, and good lighting to your new study area. Place general reading material handy in a storable container.

PROJECT SPACE

A project space doesn't need to be complicated. I use two old tables in our basement for project spaces. I love polymer clay and have allowed it to remain a staple project for the kids. The 7-foot table has been parceled off into "kingdoms," and the clay creations have taken over. The main principle in this space is to choose projects that foster the kind of skills you want your children to have—we chose to value creativity, personal initiative, dexterity, spatial awareness, and strategic thinking. What do you want to instill?

Suggestions for Creating a Project Space

Do they like to work with their hands? Include an Erector set with mechanical elements and electric motors.

Do they like to paint? Include washable paints and an easel. Make your own paint from food in your kitchen for a zero-waste fun project (see page 186).

Are board games their passion? This might be a space to host a board game. We love playing Axis and Allies with our kids for the history lessons.

How much mess am I willing to tolerate? Be honest and don't apologize if there are some activities that you can't handle. LEGOs are not allowed at my house, nor are markers or balloons. Childhood can still be amazing without these common kid items!

I find that project space works best if projects don't have to be taken down each night. This may not be possible in your home. If necessary, have your children save their project in a container with a lid.

CLOSET SPACE

Design their clothing space, closet, or dresser for self-service. I find that shelves work better for younger children because they can easily reach items without opening and shutting drawers. Label where items should go even if your child isn't reading yet. As they learn to read, they'll identify the words faster since they've seen these labels their whole life. I recommend hanging their shirts. I love Marie Kondo's style of folding, and you're welcome to check it out in the additional resources on page 185, but with six kids, it never lasts in my household. Just make sure that shelving units are bolted to the wall and that you provide a step stool for children to safely reach items.

Creating a Child's Capsule Wardrobe

Create a spreadsheet for Creating a Child's Capsule Wardrobe (page 179) for each child in your household. This sheet will help you determine a list of clothing articles your child needs, the budget for those items, the brands you'd like to find, the sizes needed, and the total clothing budget per child.

FREE PLAY SPACE

This is simply open space. Don't disregard the need for this important but "empty" square footage. All children, regardless of age, need room to move, squirm, dance, do exercises and yoga stretches, or lie on the floor to read. Even in small spaces, I recommend making free play space a priority.

SLEEP SPACE

Safety is important. Can your children easily get out of bed in the night to use the restroom? What kind of bed works best for your child? Consider heat sources and airflow for your child's comfort as well.

Style & Design

Like all rooms, minimalist design varies wildly when it comes to kids' spaces. I recommend choosing themes that fit with your overall theme in the house. True to my Scandinavian roots, I adore Scandinavian-style beds, so I use platform beds with natural wood.

Starting with an idea of the design style usually starts with the bed, as that tends to be the largest piece of furniture. Remember that there is no box you need to fit your thoughts in. The bed doesn't need to have a box spring or bed frame. You can build one or use a daybed or a floor bed. Pinterest can be helpful here as you explore different bed configurations. Of course, the bed your child already has is probably fine, too, as long as it's comfortable and safe!

The second major design element is the closet and clothing storage. Reuse furniture you have if at all possible. I have tried a million different closet shelving and dresser setups, and less is always better. Right now, I use one metal beverage tub for each of my boys' pants. They hang their shirts with extra-sturdy metal hangers. (I previously tried wooden hangers, but they were quickly commandeered into swords.) Choose long-lasting items, but don't be afraid to switch if it's not working. Journal about this if you wish, or talk through the following problem-solving exercise.

Journal Activity

Make a list of creative design solutions. Your list might look like this:

Problem: My girls love to climb on the cubby bookcase in their room, and it's dangerous. I'm afraid they will fall or it will fall on them.

Solution: If you can, turn the bookcase on its side longways so it's lower. Books go in the now-lowered cubbies, and if it's sturdy enough, the girls can sit on the top to read without getting hurt. Bolt the bookcase to the wall with two-by-fours.

Problem: My children don't want to go to bed and are afraid of the dark. They want every light on but then can't get to sleep.

Solution: Take out the blinds and install cotton curtains. Rearrange the children's beds so they can look out the window at the stars, city lights, or lightning bugs at night. Read books like *Hush Little Baby* by Sylvia Long (a great minimalist-style book) if age-appropriate, and bring in a comfy chair for you to sit and read bedtime stories. Older children can also read their own book while you read yours. Install a soft non-LED nightlight and remove any computer screens or additional tech lights that can disrupt night-time rhythms.

Children of all ages will enjoy having a role in the design process. Give them set parameters for decor to guide them. Perhaps they can reuse pictures from an old calendar to decorate their walls. Maybe give your child a pegboard to display inspirational quotes, family pictures, or letters from friends. Event tickets or memorable maps from vacation are some items that my children have wanted to keep front and center. Let them choose their favorites and release the rest. I let my daughter use Christmas lights in her room all year long. It doesn't have to cost a lot of money to make it fun for your child. Remember to celebrate your finished space with a reward you can all enjoy, and snap an "after" photo to marvel at the transformation.

Your children may be excited at this point to help you tackle the next space with gusto! Your living room is another area where their participation can be helpful, and that's where we're headed next. Keep that decluttering momentum rolling in your home with positive encouragement for everyone involved. Be patient with other household members as they get used to the transformation. Don't forget to self-congratulate! You may not be where you want to be quite yet, but enjoy and celebrate what you've done so far!

FIVE

Living and Family Rooms

"That house . . . was a perfect house. . . . Merely to be there was a cure for weariness."

—JRR TOLKIEN

The communal spaces of homes pose unique challenges when decluttering and yet also often provide the most satisfying transformations, as they create a place of rest and rejuvenation for all. Since these rooms often take up the most space in a home, they present an opportunity for family members to feel like they are an active participant in the decisions and design.

Where to Start?

Let's get planning! You'll apply the same process here as you did to the kids' rooms. Start your journal list of what's working well in the main living spaces of your house. Add notes on what's not working or what frustrates you or others.

Journal Activity

This journal entry might look something like this:

We have too many pieces of furniture in this space. I trip over the coffee table, and I don't like books, movies, newspapers, and shoes in the space. I like curling up on the couch with those I love, and the view of the sunset from the window is my favorite. I'd like this space to be cozy, clean, modern, fresh, and welcoming.

Next, in your journal, draw a rough shape of the living room, making note of windows, doorways, and heating vents. Draw dots for footprints through the space to illustrate how people walk in and out of the room. Make sure to include all entrances and a focal point in your rough sketch. Spend some time actually sitting in the room with your journal, and think through the geometry of it until you have a mental map of the space.

Questions to Ask

It's helpful to write a list of family activities that take place in these spaces. Consider the following questions:

- What do we like to do best in this room?
- Do we watch TV together?
- What furniture are we not using?
- Do we use this space for homework?
- Are there toys stored here for children or grandchildren?
- Is this a place that we would like to use to host guests?
- What's working great in this room?
- What could use fine-tuning?
- What else do we want to use this room for?

Our living room used to be the catch-all area for toys and technology. A disaster zone of epic proportions, there were playing cards, crayons, and plastic riding toys scattered everywhere. My kids enjoyed playing "52 pick-up," which only involved throwing all the playing cards up in the air and laughing as they fell to the floor. It was not a good game.

Perhaps toys aren't the problem at your house—maybe work papers cover all the surfaces. Or maybe it's technology items, such as laptops, tablets, or remote controls, that clutter every open spot. Whatever the predominant item is, make a note in your journal to tackle that first.

Journal Activity

Your journal entry might look something like this:
Living Room—frustrating clutter (in order of priority)
- Work papers and technology

- Clean laundry to be folded while watching TV
- DVDs/movies
- Dirty dishes
- Tech items, chargers, and remote controls
- Books
- Toys
- Work manuals
- Notebooks, pens
- Periodicals
- Shoes
- Unopened mail or advertisements
- Mementos from travels
- Items or gifts that don't hold value

Sorting and Logistics

The living room will require the same process of sorting and logistics as you've used in other spaces in your home. Here especially, you may want to share this four-step process with household members.

Step 1: The First Pass
Timer Set: 15 minutes

Materials Needed

1 black trash bag for trash

1 black trash bag for donating

1 Recycling Tub

1 to 4 plastic Delivery Tubs for other locations in your home

Decluttering Journal and pen

Decluttering Chart (page 173)

Uplifting music or podcast

Phone for "before" photo

Water bottle and snack for each participant

Snap your "before" photo. Grab your Decluttering Chart (page 173) to make an X for each item eliminated. Most living rooms tend to have less trash or recycling unless there are periodicals that the household subscribes to. People might also open mail here. Consider moving this "station" to your home office area, or place a recycling basket near the area where you open mail.

These rooms may be used to host holiday gatherings or family get-togethers. As you do a quick first pass and tidy-up, ask yourself: Does this living room work for both the daily activities and the occasional special events? Always think of how your house will be for holidays and large gatherings. If you declutter now, hosting company later will be much more pleasant.

In this first step, start by gathering each person's personal items. I like to use labeled baskets for each person's personal items. This might include their favorite pens, school notebooks, tablets, or headphones—things that don't yet have an assigned spot. All of it goes into each person's basket. Keep it near where the person left it if they are not present for this step in case they come looking for it later. Try to stay positive if you have clutter-loving people in your household!

Keep your journal handy as you go through this first pass, and note problem areas and solutions. For example, my kids love composition notebooks for writing and drawing in. However, they always left them on the floor near the couches. This was a tripping hazard, and I got tired of picking them up. My solution was to have them turn in a previous notebook before they got a new one. This solution serves two purposes: One, I get to see their progression in writing and drawing as we review them together; two, it honors the rule of "finish what you have before you can have more." I also gave each child a dedicated shelf inside a decorative cupboard where they could store their notebook when not in use.

Step 2: The Big Sort
Timer Set: 15 to 45 minutes per session with 2 to 10 sessions

Materials Needed

1 black trash bag for trash

1 tub or black trash bag for donating

1 plastic Sell Tub

1 Recycling Tub

1 plastic tub for items to be given away to specific people

1 to 4 plastic Delivery Tubs for other locations in your home

Decluttering Journal and pen

Decluttering Chart (page 173)

Uplifting music or podcast

Labeling supplies

Water bottle and snack for each participant

Grab your Delivery Tub, your Donate bag and Sell Tub, and your labeling kit. You'll need your full attention to make strategic decisions. You may have an abundance of technology, sports-related paraphernalia, and family heirlooms and antiques displayed in your living room and/or family room. Be gentle with yourself to avoid decision fatigue! Start at one entryway to the room, and work your way around the room until you arrive back at the same doorway, sorting all the way through. Make sure to include any furniture in the middle, such as coffee tables.

You may invite family members to help you, or you may prefer to work alone. Communicate your vision ahead of time, and schedule it on the household calendar so everyone knows the task at hand. Remind them the morning of your set decluttering time.

Initially, I decluttered alone. My husband said, "Do what you want, just don't touch my stuff!" I agreed and decluttered around him, tidying papers but not moving them. I like to call it dividing the "realm of authority" for each person but without nagging the other person. Ask once if you can help them organize and then don't ask again. You can show them the location of the donation bag and provide labeling supplies or trash bags as appropriate. Then leave it. Know that it may be weeks (or months) before they take care of their "realm of authority." It will take self-discipline on your part, but it's important to allow your adult family members the time and space to address their own clutter. Clean around it, but don't declutter for them unless they ask for help. Even then, use extreme caution and invite them to do it together.

As you sort and declutter, you'll want to consider both large- and small-impact items. You might not have any "unused" furniture, but you could think in terms of how often you use each piece. If an item is used only 20 percent of the time, is there another item that could take over that task? Can you live without it? This step will require household participation and discussion. Talk about it while you are calm and not actively sorting.

You can test out eliminating small furniture items in this step. Extra end tables, extra ottomans, coffee tables, and small miscellaneous furniture can be stashed or scooted into another room to see how you like the layout. Roll up rugs. Take curtains down or even eliminate blinds altogether. I think the concept of temporarily removing items works especially well in living rooms and family rooms, as it will help reveal what you truly need and enjoy design-wise in these spaces.

Step 3: Deliver/Sell/Donate

At this stage, delivering items will start to feel a bit easier since hopefully you have the kids' rooms decluttered and your home office space simplified. Don't worry if the influx of items from the living room seems to flood your completed spaces. This is all a part of the process, and you'll have time to refine your systems later. In this step, focus solely on the living room and/or family room.

Deciding on items to sell in this space should be a family discussion, as communal items like couches, hutches, or family antiques may come into consideration. If there's conflict over an item, wait to decide what to do with it. You want to all be in unison to avoid blame and resentment in the future. Selling large items also requires a bit of strategy and preparation. I recommend listing items for sale on Fridays and on the first of the month, since most people receive their paychecks then. Receive cash only or use the Venmo app for immediate payment, and have helpers on hand to lift furniture into vehicles if needed.

If you decide to donate items, the same strategy is required. Call ahead to note the dates and times that donations are received. This often changes, so don't depend on what's listed on the charity's website. You'll want to bring help for unloading at the charity, as many don't have enough volunteers to move heavy objects.

Some charities also offer pickups of donations, depending on where you live.

If you need to throw away large items, call your trash hauling company and ask about bulk pickup. They will provide rates, times, and dates for removal.

Some of the items you may donate or eliminate from the living room include the following:

- Coffee table
- Extra seating
- Mismatched glass vases for flowers
- Excess decorations, like candleholders, trinkets, or dried flowers
- Artwork that doesn't work
- Throw pillows that are worn-out
- Rugs
- Broken baskets
- DVDs
- CDs
- Books
- Toys
- Dog toys
- Entertainment center

You'll notice a mix of large and small items in this list. Look around your space—your list will be unique to your household.

Step 4: Tracking and Celebrating

The fun of tracking items that you declutter is that *you* get to make the rules! If you haven't used it yet, the Decluttering Chart (page 173) is graph paper filled with 500 blocks. Place an X in a block for each item or piece of furniture decluttered. Make sure to set a goal for the number of items you want to donate. A bigger item can be worth more. When I decluttered the coffee table, I gave myself 5 X's, and for the entertainment center, I gave myself 10 X's. As the chart filled up, my motivation increased and I started to see how easy it was to really make a difference.

You also may want to refer to your original timeline from chapter 2 when you put goals on your calendar. How are your time frames working for you? Did you declutter rooms faster than you thought? Do you need to adjust your expectations, as it may be taking longer to decide on sentimental items? Your timeline is a tool to serve you; go ahead and adjust it.

Celebrate your goals in tangible ways. Depending on your amount of clutter, a reasonable goal for the living room or family room might be to get rid of 100 items. You can break this down even further to five items per day, if that feels more manageable. Concurrently track your spending so that you don't self-sabotage your progress by bringing more clutter into the space. When you meet that goal, choose an activity that you wouldn't normally do—perhaps visit the art museum in the city or spend an evening at a five-star restaurant. Make the activity meaningful and memorable. You've worked hard to get to this point, so celebrate. Even though your space isn't quite done yet, you've accomplished so much, and the final reveal is coming!

Saying Goodbye to Stuff

What things should you get rid of? Please know that you don't need to get rid of everything in order to have a calm living space. Part of creating this peace will be rooted in the uniqueness of your family.

Is your family typically loud and boisterous like mine? Let go of items that don't work for your family's personality or activities. Glass items in my living room had to go! Is your family quieter and more artistic? Keep items that reflect those more sensitive principles. Glass art sculptures might be perfect for you.

Be sure to get rid of items that don't fit in the space (too big or the wrong shape). Make sure to clear space away from heating vents and anything that could block smoke detectors and carbon monoxide detectors.

Release any items with negative associations. I got rid of books that made me feel guilty for not reading them. Be free to let go of items that are part of a set. I donated matching pillows that came with couches and split up a set of lamps. It broke apart the set, and yet it worked better for my space. If it works better for you, go ahead and change the furniture to meet your specific needs.

WARNING: OBSTACLE AHEAD!

A household member might bring home more clutter right after you hit a decluttering goal. Plan on this happening at least once in this journey, and don't overreact (like I often did in the beginning!). Be patient and take deep breaths. Once you're calm, offer to help find a spot for it, and look at this as an opportunity to grow together. It's not malicious on their part, and it will likely open up new insight into your household dynamics.

If you have grief from saying goodbye to an item, shift your perspective by giving yourself a different reward! I decided to plan a fun activity each time I dropped off items at the local charity. I would schedule it so that I would drive straight from the charity to a local park. This became a habit that my children looked forward to—they were no longer focused on what we were donating but on the fun activity afterward.

SUSTAINABILITY TIP:

Fun Earth-Friendly Activities:

1. Volunteer at a local park or nature preserve.

2. Tour your recycling center.

3. Hike at state parks.

4. Take a local wildlife class on conservation efforts.

5. Take a class on native plants or maple sugaring.

6. Visit a natural history museum.

7. Pick fruit at a local farm.

8. Visit a local petting zoo—goats are the best!

9. Experience a bird or nature event. We have a hummingbird feeding event near us. (The birds will eat right out of your hand—it's magical!)

Saying goodbye to clutter is much easier when you are also saying "hello!" to new experiences.

Own Less, Live More

Less tech and more nature brought tremendous relief to our household. After I got rid of my kids' DVDs in the living room, I didn't even think to look up movies online to entertain them. I instead took this opportunity to take them outside! This epiphany came from one particular day when in total desperation I took my tantrum-throwing toddler outside and plopped him down in the grass outside our back door. He immediately stopped screaming and started to clutch the grass with his fingers and giggle, pulling up handfuls of grass. He played happily in the grass for almost an hour. I cried in relief, sitting on the steps in awe. I'd found the answer! From that point on, we removed all screens and donated all the kids' movies. We didn't do this as punishment. We cast the vision that we wanted to spend more time together and added piles of new library books to enjoy together. It took a couple of weeks, but the children quickly adjusted to a much happier routine, and the tantrums disappeared with an evening walk outside. We spent time together as a family talking over the events of the day, and the quiet was priceless.

Questions to Ask

Ask yourself thoughtful questions and set your future self up for success:

Can you cut down your time watching TV or eliminate it entirely? Keep a notebook and pen with a list of topics you'd like to learn about, located in the same container as the remote. Instead of watching TV to relax, add to the list or start learning about the items on your list by choosing books or documentaries on the topic. The goal here is to avoid mindless media consumption!

Instead, watch and read only topics you intentionally choose to pursue.

Do you want to read more? Keep books in your most comfy spot of the couch, add a reading light, and keep your reading glasses there.

Do you want your kids to read more? Keep quality children's books on low shelves that they can access. Take them to the library as a reward for decluttering!

Do you want to spend more quality time together as a family? Take the lead on suggesting fun alternatives. Go around the table and share something good or hard about your day and offer encouragement. Build a fort out of blankets and chairs in your newly decluttered living room. Or pretend the electricity's out, light some candles, and break out a deck of cards.

Do you want to spend more time with your partner? Even if you don't have a sitter, plan one evening to have your own quiet dinner together at home. If they're old enough, offer the kids their own special kids-only dinner in another room!

Do you want to spend more time in nature? Find quality walking shoes and keep them by your entryway so you're ready to take a daily adventure, even if it's only around the block.

Attachment and Sentiment

The living room holds strong emotions and memories, as this room is often where the family gathers together to relax or to host guests. Because of this, you want to be aware of the emotions that may come up for you and your family members in decluttering this space.

Feelings Checklist

Feelings you may experience as you declutter through your main living areas:

- **Excitement** as it's all coming together
- **Distress** as the mess gets bigger
- **Hope** with each item leaving
- **Invigorated** as you clear out the space
- **Exhausted** as your furniture is heavy
- **Nostalgia** as you remember all those family gatherings

Add your own insights into what emotions come up as you curate your belongings. Talk it through with one another. Pay special attention to feelings of despair or conflict with family members. Always ask for professional help if you need it, and give yourself healthy breaks from decluttering.

Reimagining Your Space

It's time to reimagine your living room and family room using the skills you've learned in the previous rooms. Think through how your other rooms came together and consider similar solutions here.

Picture Your Perfect Room

The challenges you may face in redoing your living space will be countered by the satisfaction you'll feel when it's finished! Our log home has some pretty severe design challenges, with our open floor plan and heavy tree canopy. The Realtor who showed us the house quipped that it was a small space for a family of five. The neighbor told us after we bought it that our house had sold multiple times in a few years because "it was a dark and cold home." With a few minor changes, we have more than enough space for our family of eight, and it's bright, cozy, and warm. Each home will have its own unique set of limitations. Use this opportunity to look for creative solutions!

One of the best ways I've found to solve design challenges is to ask the right questions online, such as on Pinterest. My questions included "How to brighten a log home?" and "How to live simply in small spaces?" Another solution is to think of the big picture—if you have a separate living room and family room, decide at the start of the design process what the functions in those rooms are. You may find that a formal living space is better used as an office, playroom, or music room. What works best for your family may not be what the original architects intended, and that's completely fine. Your current design style might also need to change to work with your newly decluttered space. Do the following journal activity and make notes for both the living room and family room.

Journal Activity

Go back to your Decluttering Journal and review what you previously wrote on how you wanted your home to feel. Have your feelings changed from when you first started decluttering in chapter 1? Focus here on what kind of design style you most gravitate toward. This may not match what is actually in your house right now, and that's all right. I started out with a bold Victorian style with florals and bright reds but landed on a more neutral palette in the end.

Edit your journal entry now and make notes in the margins. It might look something like this:

Current Design: Boho/hippie with bright colors and eclectic mixes of textures

Future Design: neutral palette with a white base color and only one vibrant accent color, natural textures remain

Allow your design style and yourself to change.

New Uses for New Spaces

New space in your living areas will open up new possibilities. Finding new uses for old items is my favorite design trick. I painted our hideous vintage camelback trunk white and repurposed it for wood storage for winter heating. We had decided to free up space by removing a cumbersome and large wood pellet stove and added a much smaller, more environmentally friendly high-efficiency wood stove. We then needed something to hold wood, and the trunk was the perfect size.

Minimalist Concept
Don't apologize for changing your style, your choices, or your needs.

Open space itself is a design element and will give you and your family more room to move around. Another possible way to create new space is to switch spaces entirely. One of my clients hung a salvaged door in the parlor in order to change it into a first-floor bedroom. She turned the dining room into a living room, and once she switched out the overhead lamp pieces, it aligned more with the modern look she wanted as opposed to the vintage feel of the original Victorian layout.

Be able to laugh at yourself and try new things; experiment and don't worry about failing. I tried six different couch covers over the years; I even tried to build a couch out of an old door. It didn't work. The failed "door couch" is now a favorite family story, and I learned a ton in the process—mainly that I can't be trusted with power tools.

Many living rooms have shelving of some sort. I enjoy looking at actual spaces in Restoration Hardware and Crate & Barrel for design inspiration. New ideas can come from analyzing what you like and don't like in retail stores. Note how the shelves are styled with balance and simplicity. Can you shop your home for similar symmetry and create better usage of shelving?

In your living room and family room design, don't forget the family pets. Do they have a space for their bed? What about their toys? You'll want to consider their patterns as well. Use items in new ways to hide their items if they become worn.

How about those pets who like to shed? Can you put on a slipcover or paint drop cloths or even a tablecloth-turned-couch-cover? Then you can put canned soup and emergency supplies under the couch and no one will ever know!

SUSTAINABILITY TIP:

Arrange your furniture for the most efficient airflow and heat transfer. This will be impacted by the kind of couches you have. Our home has forced air heat as our backup heat source, so our couches are raised with legs and have no skirting so air can circulate. If you must cover up a vent, do so as minimally as possible.

Style & Design

If you make a design-related purchase, it will probably be in this room. It could be a fresh coat of paint for the walls. In considering repainting, take into account what direction your windows face and how much light you get in different seasons of the year. You're going to want to take off all decorative items from the walls and evaluate them. The same four-step process used in decluttering other areas will also apply to decor.

MONEY-SAVING TIP:
Check with your local paint supplier for painting tips and to help you choose the correct paint for your wall composition. For example, plaster takes different kinds of paint than drywall. They also may have returned unopened paint that they sell at a discount and re-tint to a new color. It's always worth asking!

Considering your budget for redecorating, perhaps balance one large-ticket item for the most impact with two to three other smaller upgrades at most. Make a list before you purchase anything and consider zero-waste options whenever possible. For example, refinish hardwood floors or paint them with porch paint instead of replacing them with carpet.

Take a step back and admire the view of your newly decluttered and redesigned space. Go out the door and come back in now that you're done to commemorate your own private "reveal"! Be sure to take "after" photos. After celebrating, head to the next chapter. The kitchen is up next!

SIX

Kitchen and Dining Areas

"Kitchens are
sacred spaces."

—LYNDA McKINNEY LAMBERT

Food is a necessary part of our lives and provides the opportunity for us to bond with one another. A simplified kitchen produces more benefits than just quick food prep. The kitchen can be a family gathering space, a place to host guests, or a peaceful refuge to cook in solitude. Whatever your household needs, the kitchen deserves significant attention. Before I switched to the minimalist lifestyle, my kitchen was severely neglected. I often walked into my kitchen, looked at the mountains of dirty dishes, and walked right back out. What should have brought joy and satisfaction in the sacred task of serving my family healthy food brought only discouragement. I didn't want to face my own lack of skills in the kitchen or the mess I'd made. Today, our kitchen functions well—it's not pristine, but it's clean and works well for our large family.

Where to Start?

Grab your Decluttering Journal and a pen, and let's make a plan.

Journal Activity

You'll be analyzing your kitchen space for this journal entry.

1. What frustrates you about your kitchen? Brainstorm everything that comes to mind. It might look something like this:
   • Not enough counter space
   • No dishwasher
   • Terrible overhead lighting with old fluorescent bulbs
   • Only two drawers
   • Dated flooring

2. Now list what you adore about your space. What positive features does your space have? It might look like this:

- Big, sturdy floor-to-ceiling cabinets
- Plenty of square footage
- Mud room right off the kitchen

Think on this and try to find something positive to say, even if you hate your kitchen. It's important not to skip this step!

Once you've listed the positive and negative aspects of your kitchen, you should start to see what the problem areas are and also what your space has to offer.

Even after we moved into our dream log home, I faced challenges in the kitchen and was surprised to find that not all my frustration disappeared. I had more counter space, but the countertops were white and stained easily. I had more drawers, but they were lower quality than my previous ones. It's sometimes helpful to create a "wish list" for your kitchen and dream of different spaces, but don't let those dreams steal your joy and creativity in the present. I wasted far too much emotional energy wishing for a different kitchen instead of working on the one that I had. Accept that you are working on the kitchen that you have right now and commit to the process. It will be exponentially better when we're done!

Sorting & Logistics

Before beginning the step-by-step process, consider who is the primary person working in the kitchen. If it's not you, set an appointment with the other adults or young adult children in your household who use this space. You'll want to include them and defer to their judgment. Resist the urge to ambush them after a long day when the kitchen is a mess! When you sit down to talk about a kitchen plan, tell them your goal is to set them up for success and make kitchen tasks easier for them. Envision the space from their viewpoint and support their decisions. Then schedule a time on the calendar to dive into step 1 if you are working together.

Minimalist Concept
My creativity is more valuable than any item.

Put food in the slow cooker for the next meal before beginning each session in this step. You'll want to have a good meal ready when each session is complete!

Step 1: The First Pass
Timer Set: 15 to 60 minutes

Materials Needed

1 black trash bag for trash

1 tub or black trash bag for donating

1 plastic Sell Tub

1 plastic Duplicates Tub

1 plastic tub for items to be given away to specific people

1 to 4 plastic Delivery Tubs for other locations in your home

Decluttering Chart (page 173)

Phone for taking "before and after" photos

Uplifting music or podcast

Labeling supplies

Slow cooker and supplies for an easy dinner to cook while you're working

Whenever I tackle a room, I always start at the entrance, take a "before" photo, and "shovel a path." It's helpful to have a clear space to work. Pick up any dirty towels, socks, toys, or briefcases and put them away. Clear the floor completely of any items so you can safely move around your kitchen. Your next stop is the kitchen sink.

Here is the time to grab your Duplicates Tub, labeling supplies, and black trash bags. Stash any duplicates from around and under the sink in this tub. This could be more than one sponge (make sure they're dry), dish soap container, spatula, measuring cups, sets of knives, or even serving dishes, pots, and pans. Next, wash every single dirty dish. Don't be discouraged if this takes extra time.

Once your sink is conquered and all dishes are clean, you can see clearly what fits into the cupboards. One common area of duplicates is food storage containers. Keep out an appropriate number of small, medium, and large containers with coordinating lids. Test this amount and put the rest in storage for a week before reevaluating.

I would place duplicate or extra kitchen items in the basement and retrieve them if I needed them. However, I was unlikely to leave the kitchen and my six children (who might flood the kitchen) to get a random measuring cup. I found I could use a coffee cup, a small jar, or a larger scoop instead of a measuring cup, and then I could keep on cooking without the inconvenience of retrieving anything from the basement. What this small exercise taught me was priceless—creativity is more valuable than any one item. Suddenly, the possibilities for multiuse items seemed endless. My need for specific-use items disappeared as I learned to trust my own creativity to see alternate solutions all around me. You can do the same!

SUSTAINABILITY TIP:

Instead of plastic water bottles, keep one stainless-steel water bottle.

As you are sorting:

- Remove any items that are broken, are completely unused, or have melted or discolored with use.
- Discard burned or worn pot holders; reserve worn dish towels for rags.
- Prioritize removing any nonstick pans that are peeling or have been overheated.
- Remove any outdated food from the cupboards and refrigerator.
- Discard broken small appliances.
- Be on the lookout for items that can be recycled or composted.

Step 2: The Big Sort
Timer Set: 20 to 60 minutes with multiple sessions as needed

Materials Needed

1 black trash bag for trash

1 tub or black trash bag for donating

1 plastic Sell Tub

1 Recycling Tub

1 plastic tub for items to be given away to specific people

1 to 4 plastic Delivery Tubs for other locations in your home

Decluttering Journal and pen

Decluttering Chart (page 173)

Uplifting music or podcast

Labeling supplies

Water bottle and snack

First, you'll want to set parameters about who is allowed in the kitchen during your decluttering. You may want other household members involved, or you may need to set hard boundaries and ask them to stay out of the way. Be honest with whatever works best for you.

Minimalist Concept
Think in terms of multiuse items.

As you are sorting, organize your kitchen with specific stations and label them. Consider a station to be a space for an adult-sized person to work. It includes enough counter space plus the cupboards nearby with the tools needed for that particular station's job.

Consider these potential stations in your kitchen:

- Coffee/tea/smoothie station: coffee maker, mugs, thermoses, coffee, tea, sweetener
- Baking station: dry goods/spices
- Snack station: fresh fruits, nuts, protein bars
- Dishwashing station: includes (if a two-tub sink) a dirty side/clean side, stainless-steel scrubby, cotton washcloth, soap
- Cutting station: cutting boards and knives on highest shelf if necessary
- Go station: compost/recycle/trash
- Medication station: daily medications and vitamins, out of reach of young children
- Tools/repair station

If an item doesn't fit into these stations or another station that you deem worthy and you still want to keep it, send the item to your storage space to await being called back into service. In this step, if you have duplicate items, opt to keep the ones that are wooden or stainless steel. Discard or donate the plastic ones.

Questions to Ask

Ask yourself the following questions when deciding if you should keep an item:

- Is it easy to clean?
- How much space does it take up versus how often I use it?
- Would I miss it?
- Why do I feel attached to this item?
- What emotion is coming up for me as I hold this item?
- Can I use something else instead of this item?
- Does anyone else use this item more than I do?
- Does it prepare food that's significant to our health?
- Am I keeping this just because it's a tool that "everyone has"?
- How much would it cost to replace this item?
- Was this a gift from a significant event?

WARNING: OBSTACLE AHEAD!

Sentimental items inhabit most kitchens. My great-grandmother's canning jars stayed, but I eventually let go of other sentimental items. Consult your partner on kitchen items that may be meaningful to extended family before you declutter.

A word on linens: Quality towels and washcloths are worth the expense! Cheap fabric disintegrates quickly and ends up producing less benefit and more waste. I use heavy-weave cotton washcloths made for the bath. I keep a laundry tub in the kitchen and wash linens daily. I designate different linens as floor rags for spills—a regular occurrence in my household. These get laundered separately for hygiene's sake. I don't use paper towels or disposable sponges. For hard scrubbing, I recommend using stainless-steel chain-mail scrubbies. They are indestructible as long as you don't put them down the garbage disposal like my kids did 10 times.

If you like the industrial look and have children, I recommend using stainless-steel dishes. Choose 18/8 or 18/10 food-grade stainless steel. This way, your kids can wash their own dishes without you worrying they'll break them. Discard plastic plates that are melted or discolored, and consider how many dishes are needed. I decided that since I struggled to keep up on washing the dishes, each person would have one plate, one bowl, and one mug. I was less strict on silverware and allowed each person to have four extra spoons and forks. If there was a dirty or missing plate, my family and I would search for the lost plate and make sure it was washed before the next meal. You can keep it fun and make it a game of hide-and-seek for the plate! You may not be ready to take the plunge to one plate per person, but how about two? You can put the rest away in storage for when you have company. The point is to experiment with how much less works for you. The goal is to bring ease and simplicity to your kitchen routines.

SUSTAINABILITY TIP:

Replace paper towels, dish sponges, hot pads, and dish-drying pads with 100% cotton cloths. I recommend using dark gray cloths for long-lasting/stain-hiding quality. Launder in hot water, hang them in ventilated areas between meals, and replace them daily. This will mean that you may have 6 to 12 washcloths, but you will have eliminated other less environmentally friendly items.

You'll want to sort your kitchen in order of the areas that you use the most. Refrigerator and stove areas typically get frequent usage. Decluttering the front of the refrigerator is often a sticking point for my clients. If you're not ready to take everything off, try leaving one "representative" of each category. Love the kids' sports photos? Choose the most recent one and put the rest in albums. Do you adore the wedding invitation to your cousin's wedding? Keep it, but recycle all the graduation cards. You may also choose to clear your refrigerator entirely by transferring the artwork to a corkboard or magnetic board in your home office space. I'm pretty certain the clean look will grow on you!

Another typical problem area is the top of the fridge. For me, this area was a catch-all for cereal boxes, half-finished art projects, and items I wanted to hide. I solved this by keeping empty glass jars on top of the fridge. Since they are glass and I don't want to break them, I'm held accountable to not put anything else there for fear of knocking them down. Make strategic choices like these, which encourage your future self to keep the area for its intended purpose.

Kitchen islands and counters are also common spaces that attract clutter. If you're not ready to completely clear the counters, think of what you use on a daily basis and keep those out. You might also opt to keep out a set number of items. Maybe start with three matching canisters of dry goods if you want those on the counter. I use half-gallon Ball brand canning jars with antique zinc lids. I also use those in my pantry for a cohesive look.

Step 3: Deliver/Sell/Donate

Next, deliver items that don't belong in the kitchen. The proverbial "junk drawer" needs special attention. Don't be overwhelmed if your junk drawer is overflowing; I used to have two! Conquering this mess came through several phases. Phase one involved delivering all the items that didn't belong, such as tools, pens, or office supplies. Phase two involved deciding what should live in the drawer and separating it by like kinds. All the pens went together, and all the small tools went together, but larger tools became their own category. The third phase was maintenance: keeping order and enforcing the guidelines. It's important to deliver items back to their respective spots after each use to maintain order and not just toss things in there when you're too busy to put something back.

I wouldn't bother selling kitchen utensils, though you can donate them if they are in good condition. The only items that may sell are expensive small appliances. See if you can return an item first. If not, regift or donate the item.

MONEY-SAVING TIP:

As you sort the pantry, consider storing all dry goods in glass jars. You'll also be able to see exactly how much of each item you have and when it's almost time to buy more.

Step 4: Tracking and Celebrating

Ask your family members to keep track of the items removed from your kitchen—this is a great way for others to get involved in the process. You can ask them to keep you company during step 2 and put them in charge of the Decluttering Chart. You may want to give them the job of selling unused appliances online. You can use the Tracking Sheet (page 178) to see what you listed it for and what it sold for. If it doesn't sell in the time frame you've allotted, donate it.

It might be easier to count what's left instead of what's eliminated. I currently have two pots, one large and one small. I have two glass mixing bowls. I have one coffee maker for my husband and a

Vitamix that is used three-plus times per day. It's easier for me to count what works for our household than to count everything that I donated in the kitchen. By this point in my decluttering journey, I just wanted it to be over. Can you relate?

It's all right if you don't want to track and instead want to push through so you can celebrate the completion of your decluttering. Look at what you have, and trust that you're making good decisions.

Saying Goodbye to Stuff

As you say goodbye to items from your kitchen, I want you to get rid of one more thing: any thoughts of shame. Almost every client I worked with identified some sort of self-inflicted or family-inflicted shame over the condition of their kitchen. It's time to forgive shaming comments. If you need help decluttering this area of the home, you have every right to ask for it without feeling guilty. This space is especially appropriate to ask for help from household members, friends, or professional organizers. Release any self-defeating thoughts and a false sense of guilt; it only slows you down.

Instead, here are affirmations to say:

Affirmation Statements

I love re-creating my kitchen.

I'm happy to get a chance to start over.

I forgive the negative comments made about my kitchen.

I'm excited to create healthy meals in my new space.

I'm choosing more zero-waste options a little bit at a time.

I know I'll learn the skills it takes to keep my kitchen simple and clean.

I'm ready for my kitchen to serve me, not the other way around.

Own Less, Live More

The benefits of a decluttered kitchen can impact every area of your life. The new stations will allow you to have an orderly flow of kitchen tasks, and being in a kitchen you adore will inspire you to cook more thoughtfully. If you don't need to fumble to find what you need, you can easily train others in your household to cook as well. Because my children can cook, I am freed up to work on other projects, and the household still gets fed. I'm so grateful to walk in the door after business meetings and see a clean kitchen with food on the table. Making space sure feels (and tastes) good!

Feelings Checklist

Stop and consider how you're feeling after all this work. You may feel:

- **Triumph** at conquering a serious amount of clutter
- **Frustration** at the sheer number of items
- **Fear** of getting rid of family kitchen items
- **Excitement** as shelves begin to open up and new possibilities appear
- **Inspiration** to cook again
- **Discouraged** at how long it is taking
- **Sadness** at letting go of useful items that never got used
- **Relief** at having a fresh start
- **Ashamed or overwhelmed** at the volume of disorder behind closed cabinets

Take out your Decluttering Journal and write your own emotional response while it is still fresh.

Reimagining Your Space

What's your vision for your kitchen? Think of how it will serve your household in this season of life. Don't worry if you've tried to update your kitchen before and find yourself reimagining your space again now that you've decluttered. Seasons change, and so have you!

Picture Your Perfect Room

I had a season in my little log home where we served a sit-down meal for 25 people on an almost weekly basis. My kitchen was set up differently than it is now. Then, my perfect kitchen held plates, serving dishes, and glasses for everyone. I no longer keep the same supplies on hand. Your kitchen changes as your needs change.

Before you rearrange your kitchen to match your current season, look for pictures of kitchens online that inspire you. My main kitchen inspiration came from Bea Johnson, author of *Zero Waste Home*. Consult websites like HGTV.com, Apartmenttherapy.com, and Decordemon.blogspot.com. Find similar layouts to your current kitchen and save only photos that provide a design feature that solves a specific question you have regarding your space. Choose elements that are aesthetically pleasing and fulfill the function of your specific stations in that part of the kitchen. Coordinate the design of the kitchen with that of adjoining rooms to provide a cohesive flow in your home.

> Minimalist Concept
> *Create and re-create rather than consume.*

New Uses for New Spaces

Since you've opened up additional space in cupboards you've decluttered, you may have extra cabinets or drawers. It's time to see new opportunities in the new spaces. For a time, we put special activities in empty lower cupboards and gave each of our children their own special cupboard.

Decluttering can also reveal new solutions. My home was designed with both a formal dining area in the living room and a kitchen dining area. At first, I had two tables but found I couldn't keep two tables clean to save my life, so I eliminated one set. With only one table in the combination dining area/living room, we had a limit to what kinds of messes we could create. I set up a much-needed entryway in place of the old table set in the kitchen. I repurposed an old piano bench for sitting to put on shoes and a coat tree for all coats and reusable grocery bags. The empty kitchen pantry cupboards near the back door now were repurposed to hold socks and shoes. My point is, get creative with the kind of entryway or lack of entryway, and see unique solutions for storage.

Maybe you have larger decisions to make. I had a client who chose to declutter her entire house instead of increasing her monthly cost and buying a bigger house elsewhere. This decluttering process led to the revelation that the current home could work long term. She chose a kitchen renovation that created much-needed space and provided additional square footage for the family to work comfortably together. With her newly redesigned island, she started teaching her teens how to cook and had neighborhood friends over for pancake breakfasts: a delicious reward for all her decluttering efforts!

Style & Design

In minimalism, there is still room for a wide variety of styles, especially in the kitchen. This room is fun to simplify and redesign because small changes can make a dramatic difference. First, take an assessment of your kitchen in the context of its physical layout in the home. What role does it play? Is it near the entry door to the house? Many kitchens are located at the rear of the structure with a side entrance. How will people come into the room, and how will you bring in groceries and remove trash?

Consider creative solutions. Put together a Pinterest board or create a vision mood board in your kitchen. You can paint stoves and hoods, remove built-in microwaves, use heavy-duty contact paper to re-cover the front of dishwashers, and put up open shelving with simple refurbished brackets. Pull together ideas, but be careful not to get lost in the possibilities. I suggest picking no more than one large DIY and several smaller DIY projects.

Minimalist Concept
Use what you have and then you can have more.

Next, play to the design strengths you have in the kitchen. Do you have great views from the kitchen window above your sink? If so, capitalize on that: Take off blinds, switch to less obstructive curtains, or remove curtains entirely. Search online for kitchens that have similar layouts, and find ways to emphasize the positive aspects of your space.

I also enjoy using the four steps we cover in each chapter on decor items. Think in terms of design styles you've explored in other rooms as you do the first pass, big sort, deliver/sell/donate, and track/celebrate. Do you have a large number of Boho or traditional-style dishes? Do you appreciate a sleek, industrial feel? Sort through your decor and see what your decorative items say about your preferences. Then ask yourself, "Does this still reflect what I think is beautiful?"

This is also time to pull back in those sentimental items that you decided to keep. You can refurbish or display them now in a way that is deserving of their importance. Think about how they work with your current design style. For example, I love the vintage feel of the antique canning jars from my great-grandmother, but I also wanted to go a bit more industrial in the kitchen. Rather than replacing the jars with modern canisters, I scored vintage zinc lids by asking around at antiques shops. The metal lids fit the industrial vibe I wanted and were a cheaper switch to keep the sentimental jars in daily use.

Quick & Easy Kitchen Updates

- Add a plant.
- Take off the hardware from cabinets and go without it.
- Paint hardware. (Rustoleum brand is the one I like for this task.)
- Remove cupboard doors.
- Remove shelves inside the cupboard.
- Add organizers to large spaces.
- Remove dividers in small spaces.
- Install under-cabinet lighting.

For larger elements, go slowly with the redesign. I recommend going neutral and timeless when choosing flooring, lighting, cabinets, appliances, and sink/faucet, since those take the most money and effort to change. If you want to go with trendy pieces, make those pieces a decorative focal point and not permanent fixtures.

WARNING: OBSTACLE AHEAD!

Before altering any structural elements in your kitchen or areas involving electric, plumbing, removing or replacing trim, or scraping paint, consult a licensed professional contractor. If your home was built prior to 1978, you'll want to make certain you don't have any lead-based paint that could be exposed.

For a bigger impact without too much expense, you can paint cabinets, countertops, and hardware. Check your Habitat for Humanity ReStore or thrift store for building items or hardware. Another money-saving move is to check with your local contractor—they often have overstocked or discontinued supplies they can sell for very low prices. Call a countertop supplier for marble countertop fragments. Look for refurbished sinks on Facebook Marketplace.

If you plan to paint the walls, ask your paint store about a combined primer and paint, depending on your walls' composition. Decide on color ratios, with 80 percent being your dominant color in the entire room, including walls, decor, cabinets, and countertop. That leaves about 20 percent for accent colors. Work with color families by choosing colors that flow naturally from room to room and come from related colors that work with your overall style. Avoid colors that clash with other colors in the adjoining rooms, with the trim, or with the flooring.

WARNING: OBSTACLE AHEAD!

While focusing on one major structural element, don't get sucked into the trap of the "while we're doing this, we might as well . . ." mentality that ends up in a whole house remodel! Knowing when to stop is just as important as knowing where to start. Decide the limits before starting the project, and make sure you and your contractors stick to it.

Once all the redesign work is done, remember to take your "after" photos and enjoy a meaningful reward. Take time to celebrate the progress you've made and keep your momentum going to the next room—the master bedroom.

SEVEN

The Master Bedroom

"A home is the perfect reflection of its inhabitant: You don't have to look too hard to see a person's essence manifest itself in the interior."

—RIEKO OHASHI

Now that you've worked through a large portion of your home, you get to practice your new skills in the master bedroom. This room poses some unique challenges. The master bedroom's main purpose is for rest and rejuvenation, a haven away from the hustle and bustle of the rest of the household. However, it can also become a serious dumping ground for clutter. Clutter here becomes "out of sight, out of mind," at least until you retreat to your room at the end of the day. My master bedroom became that way, and I was too exhausted to address it when I finally fell into bed at night.

Where to Start?

The key to conquering the master bedroom is to start before you are tired. In the morning, when you are fresh, take an objective look at your space. Consider what is working well. Take an honest look at what's not working.

Sorting & Logistics

The master bedroom is going to take a deliberate cooperative strategy—unless you're single, you'll need to declutter and collaborate with your partner or spouse. This can take patience and effort.

Step 1: The First Pass
Timer Set: 15 minutes or less

Materials Needed
2 garbage bags (1 for donate, 1 for trash)

1 plastic Sell Tub

1 clear plastic Duplicate Tub

1 or 2 clear plastic Delivery Tubs

1 Recycling Tub

Laundry baskets, empty or full

Decluttering Journal and pen

Decluttering Chart (page 173)

During this quick sort, collect any dirty coffee mugs, technology that is now stored elsewhere, and books or papers that should be in the home office. Also make a note of what kinds of clutter you're seeing on surfaces. Is it jewelry, linens, or clothing? Is it your partner's items that are in their realm of authority? Identify what types of items are tripping you up. Move quickly, decluttering like you did in the previous rooms. You won't be including your partner in this first pass, so don't touch any of their stuff. Either allow enough time to deliver items or close the lid on your Delivery Tub.

The key is to go quickly in this step—if you don't get everything delivered, that's all right.

After this sort, prepare for a restful sleep. Change the sheets and lay out your sleep clothing and anything else you need to make sleep easier tonight when you come back to this space. You might find it helpful to print out or snap a picture of the affirmations on page 7 so you can read them before bed or upon waking in the morning.

To get ready for step 2, set up a time or date night to discuss your master-bedroom strategy with your partner. Maybe you have never cleaned while angry, but I sure have! Strategy sessions about my angry-cleaning spree didn't stay calm either, but you'll make the best progress if you can rein in your passion for the cause and make your partner feel like you value their thoughts. During your strategy chat, ask them questions, listen quietly, and be ready with your Decluttering Journal to take notes.

Questions to Ask

How do you feel about our journey to simplify the house? Brace yourself for honest answers, and don't react unkindly if it's negative. Even if there is a long silence, give your partner an opportunity to process and think through what they would like to say. Try to avoid feeling offended if there's constructive criticism. Stay objective and don't take the criticism personally. Your partner may need to verbally process bottled-up emotions that you've already worked through in your Decluttering Journal. You may want to include your partner in some of the Decluttering Journal activities listed throughout the book, depending on their comfort level.

What would you like to do differently in the master bedroom? Take notes again and acknowledge their good ideas. Don't worry if you don't agree with their ideas right away. Your partner may come up with things that you don't like, but that's not the point. Your job is to listen and value their perspective. You'll have a more receptive audience for your viewpoint if you start by listening to theirs.

How can I make our master bedroom a more peaceful and restful place for you? Ask with genuine concern and listen carefully to what frustrates your partner about the space. Is it too hot? Too cold? Are they annoyed by all the clothes or tripping over your books in the night? Listen for practical items that can be fixed.

Would you like to be involved in step 2? Invite, don't insist. If they don't want to be involved, then agree on clear parameters of how you'll proceed. Determine what their preferences are, and come to an agreement of how to divvy up the tasks. If your partner wants to be involved, then set up a scheduled time on the calendar to do The Big Sort. Plan a sweet reward for completing the master bedroom together!

Step 2: The Big Sort

Timer Set: 15 to 90 minutes per session with multiple sessions as needed

Materials Needed

1 trash bag for trash

1 trash bag for donating

1 to 4 plastic Delivery Tubs

1 plastic Sell Tub

1 plastic Recycling Tub

1 plastic tub for items to be given away to specific people

Decluttering Journal and pen

Decluttering Chart (page 128)

Uplifting music or podcast

Labeling supplies

Water bottle or cup of tea and snack for each of you

Clear It Out

Don't try to conquer everything at once. Instead, set aside time for one session per category (keeping similar items together). Keep the appointment just like you would with an important colleague or cherished friend:

Clothing: daily, exercise, sleepwear, winter, summer, business, coats, boots, shoes, accessories, jewelry

Linens: bedsheets, blankets, mattress covers, pillowcases

Media: books, movies, CDs, training resources, college textbooks, exercise videos

Decor: wall art, candles, lamps, knickknacks, plants, picture frames

Sentimental Items: gifts from family, any items with strong emotion attached

Don't pull out more than one category per session. If something is in another category, leave it alone or set it aside in your Decluttering Command Center until your scheduled "appointment" with that category.

Help things go smoothly in The Big Sort:

- Remember that your partner may not have gone through the same emotional and mental process that you have.
- Give extra grace and keep your expectations low.
- Watch your partner's frustration level.

- Learn their sense of categories and keep your own frustration in check.
- Respect their autonomy and realms of authority.
- Be ready to compromise when needed.

WARNING: OBSTACLE AHEAD!

Not every compromise needs to be 50/50 in order for it to be a workable solution. If your spouse is a saver and you are not, you may want to give them more space for their items. It doesn't need to be the same amount of space as you have in order for it to be a workable solution. Create healthy boundaries. For example, your boundary may be that you need a clear space to get to the bathroom at night without tripping, but you can ignore the piles of books on their side of the bed. Keep your ultimate goal as your focus and allow for multiple solutions. Decluttering this room is about maintaining a healthy bond with your partner while creating minimalism to the best of your ability.

Many organizers recommend pulling everything out at once in a bedroom. I've done this in my own room; it was an explosion of junk and clothing and a recipe for disaster! I recommend pulling out only one category at a time. The most popular category to sort first is clothing.

Creating an Effective Laundry Room

While we're on the subject of clothing, let's detour to the laundry room for a moment. As you work to eliminate excess clothing, you can also take steps to make sure your laundry room is equipped to do its best work for the clothing you choose to keep and wear.

Evaluate the laundry area. Is there anything that can be decluttered, improved, fixed, or rearranged? Small changes can make a large impact. Start by listing your essentials. As an example, here are mine:

- Borax for hard water and stain removal
- Laundry detergent
- Dr. Bronner's Sal Suds for grease stain removal
- Scrub brush
- Small container for items found in pockets to deliver else-where in the home
- Iron and ironing board
- Small sewing kit

You may choose to locate house cleaning supplies near the laundry. I call this my Cleaning Station, and I chose to make most of my own cleaning supplies from a few multiuse ingredients (see page 188 for my favorite sources for recipes).

MONEY-SAVING TIP:

Buying cleaning supplies in bulk saves money and makes budgeting easier. I set aside an amount each month so that I can purchase a year's worth of dish soap. That may seem like a lot, but it saves money per ounce and also saves needing to remember to purchase it during weekly grocery runs. Track usage by writing the date opened on the bottle cap of the larger gallon container with a permanent marker and then pouring small amounts in the bottle that is used daily at the sink.

Step 3: Deliver/Sell/Donate

Now that you've sorted and decided what to keep and let go of in your bedroom, this is where all of the pieces of the puzzle go into place. You've gotten the routine down of delivering, selling, and donating items. Your home may not match your vision 100 percent quite yet, but you're working toward it. You should be able to find and put things away somewhat easier than when you first began.

By this step, there's probably less that needs to be put away in the rest of the house. You've also created systems and stations so you already know where items should go. It all has a home and a designated space if it's supposed to be in the other rooms in your house. You've made the choice to stop buying more and instead sell or donate items. The Sell Tub should be emptying out as things are sold and the money deposited into your reward account. You may want to look into the Venmo app for any garage sales you'd like to host. With Venmo, people can purchase the item and pay via credit or debit card instantly through the app. And as you donate more items, the local charity may start to know your name—this is a good feeling! Remember your Decluttering Chart on page 173, and place an "X" in the boxes on the graph to chart your progress.

The hardest category in decluttering the master bedroom for me was clothing; I wasn't sure what I would need. I have gained and lost over 270 pounds (45 pounds per child times 6 kids), so my needs have certainly changed quickly. I lost the weight with each child just in time to have another baby! It's time to build a capsule wardrobe for yourself even if you have a fluctuating weight. A capsule wardrobe is an intentional set of basic clothing that doesn't go out of style and can have rotating accessories or accent pieces. Normally, the number of essential articles of clothing would be small enough to provide easy decision-making but large enough to accommodate different activities. Building a capsule wardrobe takes time upfront, but it saves so much time and mental energy in the long run that it's worth the effort.

Build a Capsule Wardrobe

Here's how:

1. **Deliver clothing that doesn't currently fit to a storage spot.** Keep only those items that are your favorites but bigger or smaller than you are right now. Give preference to natural fabrics that don't need dry-cleaning. Poshmark and thredUP are two companies that make selling clothing online easy. If the clothing has never fit quite right, even if it's expensive and name-brand, either sell or donate it. Your clothing should serve you and fit you comfortably.

2. **Evaluate the clothing that fits today.** Don't worry if your size is changing quickly. Focus on right now. Pull out all pants and shirts for the appropriate season, such as winter or summer.

3. **Look for color patterns.** What colors make you feel confident and happy? What colors are practical for your tasks? Remember when we talked about the jobs your rooms complete? Now you'll list your own jobs so that you can match your clothing to it. Author Kim Brenneman recommends matching your clothing to the particular job you do each day of the week.

Consider your many roles. For example, here are mine:
- Homeschool mom/wife
- Business owner—financial and minimalist coach
- Educator/public speaker—financial and insurance education
- Runner

Most people need essential multiuse and base items for the different roles you may play each day. For example, I have black shirts and comfortable slacks that I can easily throw a suit jacket over as I run out the door, switching from homeschooling to a business meeting. After the meeting, I go for a run, changing only my shoes. When I'm speaking at a conference, I can easily attend to my toddler with the babysitter in between speaking sessions because my suit jacket is washable and can be quickly spot-cleaned. All my clothing is comfortable and allows me to move freely. I'm not getting any awards for being a fashionista, but the clothing works for me and doesn't distract from my purpose and tasks in each role. What style works for you and your daily activities?

4. **Select your most versatile pieces first.** For example, I have a black pair of pants that I can wear for all four of my roles. They are the top priority to keep. Next, I have pants that work for three out of four. That's how I prioritize clothing decisions in

addition to condition and fabric composition. You'll know that you've decluttered enough clothing when you can easily keep up on laundry and feel confident in your daily clothing choices. "Enough" clothing isn't a specific number; rather, it's unique to what works for you in this season of your life.

Step 4: Tracking and Celebrating

Are you keeping track on your Decluttering Chart as you donate? You're making great progress, and tracking that progress will help you stay focused and strong throughout this journey. You may evaluate your decluttering sessions, schedule a whole weekend to complete a Quantum Sprint decluttering session, or set the next reward on the calendar. Involve your household in tracking and celebrating the journey, whether they've been actively helping or just "helping" by giving you your space. Perhaps you're ready to host guests to celebrate. Be intentional and share why you are celebrating and all that you've been working toward. Don't apologize that you've still got more work to do or that your house isn't "perfect." Just enjoy the moment!

Saying Goodbye to Stuff

The master bedroom is often a lesser-traveled space in a home and therefore tends to contain breakable objects or old items perhaps from childhood. As you craft a restful space, be attentive to what emotions come up in relationship to physical items.

Sometimes the sheer volume of items can cause a sense of emotional paralysis. If you're having trouble seeing categories, you may have decision fatigue and feel stuck saying "goodbye." One way to remedy this is to ask your item, "Where is your home?" Holding an item in your hands and focusing only on that item blocks out the other items you may feel are demanding your attention.

Other questions that can help you become unstuck include: Where do I use this item most? How long have I had this item? If I had to replace this, how much would it cost? Will I care about this item next year if it's gone?

You can shift the paralysis with simple questions and focused actions zeroed in on one item at a time. You can also gain tremendous power to work past the feeling of "stuck" by speaking affirmations aloud as well as taking actions. Read over the Affirmation Statements on page 7. You may also need to physically get up from your sorting to do stretches or take a walk outside.

As you walk through the decision-making process, you are actually creating new cognitive pathways for making future decisions. Slowing down is beneficial. I know that one of my clients didn't want to go through items that reminded her of a family member who had recently passed away. She was physically and emotionally exhausted by grief. Taking extra time to work through whatever feelings you have before deciding what to do with emotional items is absolutely appropriate! Having a chart like the Decluttering Chart (page 173) provides a plan and plots out the end decision so you can (1) track the logical progression of things, and (2) feel confident that you made the right decision without second-guessing yourself.

In the master bedroom, I found that I was keeping gifted items that brought up frustration and sadness for me. Whenever I walked into the room, I felt waves of negative emotions at the gifted decor I didn't ask for. For example, I held on to a gift that made me feel sick at the extravagant cost. I was given this expensive item and meanwhile I was struggling to find money to feed the children. I didn't know what to do! I didn't want to offend anyone, but I eventually decided to sell the item, and I was relieved. That experience gave tremendous insight into a problem area I needed to resolve for myself. I was keeping an item, for more years than I'd like to admit, for fear of what that person would say. When I identified that, I could see how ridiculous my decision had been. Get rid of items that produce false guilt! Release responsibility that is not yours. Be free to forgive anyone who has offended you, forgive yourself for keeping it if needed, and let go of the item.

The main concept here is that eliminating items is freeing. Without guilt, you aren't weighed down. You can then use your creativity to design your room. What makes you feel happy and whole? Display that special photo from a memorable trip; welcome soft natural fabrics that speak of sustainability. Welcoming and releasing is a necessary cadence of coming to a place of rest, especially in this intimate space of the home.

Own Less, Live More

Just like you've done in other spaces in the house, make it easy on your future self to maintain the simplicity you've created. The benefit of owning less in the master bedroom is that you'll no longer allow it to become the dumping group for household clutter. There was a mental shift that happened for me. As a woman and a mother, I had for too long felt that my master bedroom personified me; I was a dumping ground for others' bad decisions. I absorbed negativity and responsibility for others' choices, and it manifested itself in the mountains of unwearable gifted clothing and decorative items I didn't want. I didn't feel worthy of setting healthy boundaries because I had never seen it done, physically or emotionally. When I took back my master bedroom and created a haven for myself and my husband, I also took charge of what items would occupy my master bedroom going forward!

You may be able to relate but in a different way. Perhaps you lack storage and so your bedroom hosts all the toys, artwork, and papers that won't fit anywhere else. Whatever stands between you and your restful haven, it will be lessened by the decluttering process and by making the same kinds of "let it go" decisions.

Establishing this healthy boundary in both physical and emotional space can create new confidence and strength within you as it did for me. I could choose and enforce sustainable choices that aligned with my commitment to environmental stewardship. I could choose to say no to guilt-laden gifts that caused family disputes and jealousy. No more drama allowed! Now you can dive more deeply into your own personal design style without complications. For me, this opened a door to creativity that I didn't know existed, and when my master bedroom reflected my relationship with my husband alone, it became restful and life-giving. I wish the same for you!

Attachment & Sentiment

As you work through the Feelings Checklist in this room, you may want to give yourself extra time to journal. Many of my clients felt that this room contained additional layers of emotion, probably because we as human beings identify deeply with the intimate space that is a "room of our own." The items that you've decluttered and the conversations that were needed if you have a partner may be emotionally draining. But remember, you're working through the hard emotions to find a place of peace!

Feelings Checklist

Some of the feelings that may be coming up for you:

- **Nostalgia**
- **Excitement**
- **Restlessness**
- **Indecision**
- **Insecurity**
- **Inspiration**
- **Freedom**
- **Curiosity**
- **Contemplation**

Add sentences to each word you're feeling to further identify what emotions are coming up for you. You may also want to look back and see how previous checklists looked in different rooms. This exercise should give you hope as you see all that you've accomplished in growing emotional autonomy from "stuff."

Reimagining Your Space

It's time to reimagine your space and think through the major design elements that create a master bedroom. As with your other rooms, you'll want to reevaluate the jobs your room performs. Now that the clutter has been cleared, are you sure you want to keep using this space as you did before? For example, our master bedroom on the main floor actually had the smallest square footage, which was an awkward architectural design feature that was a challenge when we bought the log home. This small room also served as a home office, video studio, and closet for all eight family members. Once we decluttered, we realized that too many tasks were being crammed into our smallest bedroom! We switched our master bedroom and office/video studio to the largest bedroom upstairs and moved the boys to the smallest bedroom. You may want to do logistical changes now as you reimagine your bedroom in relationship to your residence's floor plan.

If you are a caregiver, you may need to redesign your spaces to care for aging parents or grandparents in your home. Multigenerational homes are becoming common. Should your bedroom be closer to theirs for nightly safety checks? Should you move rooms so that everyone is on the same story of a two-story house? Or can you finish the basement as a second master bedroom to make caregiving easier? Embrace your particular season of life and work with the needs of your household. You can create beautiful spaces that work for everyone as you give care to those you love!

Picture Your Perfect Room

As you create a picture of your perfect room, consider walking through at least three different retail stores' bedroom displays—not for purchase but for inspiration. You might even ask your friends to give you a tour of their master bedroom to see the layout and design. This room, more than any other, calls for your personal touch, and it helps to physically experience a room to help you discern your personal style. Watch for ideas everywhere. Magazines in doctors' offices or in a coffee shop may give you ideas. Ask on Facebook for design ideas or websites or blogs to follow, and see the Resources section on pages 187 and 188 as well.

Consider all five senses in this room. How do you want to feel when you walk in your bedroom at night? Do you want to sigh with relief that everything is clean and ready for you to rest? Your master bedroom is one of the most important rooms to fully experience because of the personal, reflective nature of having a resting place.

New Uses for New Spaces

You may find, like I did, that when I created the capsule wardrobe, I didn't even need furniture to hold clothing anymore. I could fit all my clothes on 10 hangers, and I didn't need a dresser or wardrobe to house all of my clothes.

If you find yourself in the same situation, what should you do with large pieces of furniture you no longer need? You may want to eliminate the furniture altogether. You may find other uses for the furniture in other rooms of your home. My former wardrobe became a much-needed linen closet for storing winter blankets.

In fact, we set up capsule wardrobes for our whole family, so we had significantly more space in the closet. We removed all the clothing from our master bedroom and actually created a single "family closet" in the boys' room that held all eight family members' clothing. My daughter eventually took ownership of her clothing and moved it to her room, so now we have the wardrobes of seven people in one two-by-eight-foot closet and one moderately sized dresser for my husband's additional clothing.

With the new open space, we created a space for succulents, since our master bedroom has three full walls of windows. Now we have room to propagate and re-pot various kinds of plants since we don't need any dressers for clothing.

When you eliminate excess, you may find new space for passions you've always wanted to pursue. Curate these new spaces carefully and slowly, taking into account the time and cost in adding anything into your new space.

Style & Design

As you consider new uses for your open space in the master bedroom, you'll want to have a plan for the style and design. Start with large elements, such as the bed and windows, while remembering the location of the heating elements.

Shapes and geometry matter, especially here in the master bedroom. Most bed frames are rectangular, so you might want to add visual balance by adding a circular mirror or wreath above the headboard. In arranging the bed, choose your headboard carefully or forgo it entirely. We chose a sustainably grown pine platform bed for our master bedroom without any headboard. Perhaps you'll make do with the frame and headboard that you already have, and that may work perfectly. You can also paint it with chalk paint or a three-in-one primer. Choose zero-VOC paint—this is especially important in the bedroom due to chemical fumes found in many paint products that can remain in the air for months after the paint dries. For a quick upgrade, simply change the arrangement of pillows. Add height or remove them entirely—trust your artistic taste. Try new arrangements for a week as an experiment, and enjoy the process of creating!

Like you did in the living room, you'll want to identify your focal point. Where do your eyes immediately gravitate? Does your room have high ceilings? What design elements do you adore? What drives you nuts? As you deliberately think through this room, you'll want to accept limitations without frustration and accentuate the positive. For example, I have high ceilings but small windows. I hung the curtains high above the small windows, showcasing the high ceiling and diminishing the awkward size of the windows. I also removed the broken and dated blinds. Instead, I hung white cotton twin sheets with curtain clips for curtains.

Think also about secondary lighting for bringing a calming ambience and lowering the lights at the end of the day. You may like to sit and write out your calendar for the next day before bed. If so, consider adding a lamp and reading chair. Feel free to remove bedside stands or add them to match your bed height as an attached shelf to the wall. We used TV trays for a while because they were the right height. Match your design to your actual life—too many people buy things for style without thinking about whether they function with or meet the needs of their lifestyle. Use the design to support rhythms you want to create.

As you create a space as a haven in the master bedroom, you'll be able to rest and relax enjoying the fruit of your labors. Decluttering is hard work, physically and emotionally, but having a room that is a refuge and reflects your personal style is the perfect end to a long day that you'll enjoy for a long time to come.

Now that you've completed your master bedroom, you may have other spaces to conquer that aren't listed in this book. Keep going! You have the skills to create a home that serves your purpose.

You may not live in a studio or small space such as a tiny house, but perhaps you're curious if you'd like to make that kind of switch someday. Check out the next chapter for creative ideas for people living in studio apartments and other small spaces.

EIGHT

Studio Apartments and Other Small Spaces

"Just because something
made you happy in the past
doesn't mean you have
to keep it forever."

—JOSHUA BECKER

Living more with less can be done, no matter your home's actual square footage, and in fact, the decluttering process is especially important for those in a smaller space. The decluttering in this case requires honest evaluation of what is essential to keep and what can be released.

Where to Start?

A growing number of people are choosing to live in a studio apartment, tiny house, or alternative living arrangement. Perhaps you're renting a room in someone else's house or you've opted to live in an RV. Even if you're just considering downsizing further, this chapter will help you determine what size space will work best for you.

Clutter and disorganization have a stronger impact when the space is small. In some ways, you can look at this as the ultimate minimalist canvas to start crafting only the essential things in your life. Limitations can actually produce freedom and creativity; it all depends on your perspective.

Sorting & Logistics

Be patient with yourself as you're planning your decluttering with the four-step process. You may need to make more decisions while living in a small space because you don't have the luxury of delaying choices, as do households with extra storage options. You may have skipped ahead to this chapter knowing that your studio, small living arrangement, dorm room, house share, or tiny house produces its own unique set of processes. If so, welcome, and let's get started!

Step 1: The First Pass

Timer Set: 15 minutes

Materials Needed

1 black trash bag for trash

1 black trash bag for donating

1 plastic Delivery Tub

1 plastic Sell Tub

1 plastic Recycling Tub

1 plastic tub for items to be given away to specific people

Decluttering Journal and pen

Decluttering Chart (page 173)

Uplifting music or podcast

Labeling supplies

Water bottle or cup of tea and a snack

Journal Activity

Grab your Decluttering Journal. For items and furniture that you are considering decluttering and weighing out if they are worthy of storage, there is a helpful equation. One way to find whether an object is worthy of keeping is to find out how much it costs to use the space that item requires:

monthly housing cost (rent or mortgage plus taxes, utilities, insurance) / home's square footage

=

monthly cost per square foot

Now, how large is the item or furniture in question? If it's a six-foot couch, you would multiply your monthly cost per square foot times six feet to get your monthly "cost" to store your couch.

List any items that can be reduced in size (such as a smaller microwave, space-saving bed, folding table, etc.). This will reduce the monthly "cost" of storage but continue to accomplish needed tasks.

When you're working with a small space, it can be especially daunting knowing where to start. Your hot water heater may fill what once had been closets. As you're doing your first pass, you may not have the traditional storage options of a framed house. You may also have to think in terms of zones instead of rooms.

When you're doing a big sort in a small space, it can create an enormous mess. For this reason, I recommend sorting by zones and routines, and only tackling one zone per session. For example, in the first step, sort the items associated with your Go Routine. This would include shoes, briefcase, reusable grocery bags, library books, recycling, keys, sunglasses, and jackets. Consider the weather in how you can strategically use multiuse items to reduce the amount of storage you need. For example, instead of having two different kinds of boots, we use rain boots in the spring for muddy days and the same boots in the winter snow with thick wool socks.

Place any items that need delivery to other zones in your Delivery Tub now. Stay focused only on this zone by placing out-of-place items into this tub that you will deliver at the end of this first step. Leave enough time at the end to deliver the items to other zones as appropriate.

In this first pass, you'll also want to grab any unopened mail, recycling, trash, or dirty dishes. Since your space is small, you may find many items are out of place because they don't have a place. Add those to your Delivery Tub. Stash any items that should be donated in the black trash bag for donations.

Zones you may need to address based on your space and routines:

- Go zone (entryway and any items that frequently go with you)
- Kitchen zone
- Office zone
- Sleep zone
- Pet zone
- Clothing/laundry zone

Step 2: The Big Sort

Timer Set: 15 to 90 minutes per session with multiple sessions as needed

Materials Needed

1 black trash bag for trash

1 black trash bag for donating

1 plastic Delivery Tub

1 plastic Sell Tub

1 plastic Recycling Tub

1 plastic tub for items to be given away to specific people

Decluttering Chart (page 173)

Uplifting music or podcast

Think of items that can be reduced in size or modified—you can get super creative with regard to beds. Murphy beds or trundle beds can prove exceptional space savers. We currently use a trundle bed with our boys and love it! Apartmenttherapy.com recommends adding wheels to your furniture in order to move it easily throughout a normal day or weekly cycle of living. Remember the option that you can add wheels before you get rid of any furniture that you'd like to keep. If you share the space with a partner or roommate, be sure to include them in The Big Sort and see page 129 about questions to ask them as you begin the process of working together.

In small closets, you can hang more than one piece of clothing on the same clothes hanger. For example, belts can be hung on the same hanger as the pants that go with it. Lightweight T-shirts can all be hung on the same hanger since they aren't heavy. Use sturdy metal clothes hangers that match. It looks better, and it also makes the clothing slide and fit together better in the closet. Consider creative solutions to make your closet bigger. I took the closet doors off our family closet entirely, and it opened up the room and space by several additional inches.

You may not have closets at all. That brings its own challenges, but it's also a great opportunity. Consider garment racks or wardrobes that can double as a bookshelf on top. Look for how to display clothing like in a retail store, hanging like kinds of garments together. Conversely, consider placing items together not by type but by color. Experiment with what looks best to your eye, and arrange it near other color-coordinating furniture if possible. This is helpful to discern which items to keep and which to eliminate, because you'll see how the items look within the space constraints of your room.

As you sort, you may find items that have been lost for a long time. Create a new location for that item so it doesn't get lost again. The same principle applies as you go through your Delivery Tubs. If an item doesn't have a designated "home," create one now. Even if it's not perfect or permanent, designate and label that spot.

MONEY-SAVING TIP:

When you can easily find items by keeping like items together, you'll eliminate the cost of buying duplicate items. For example, if you keep all the light bulbs together, you can keep track and avoid overspending, and stock up when items are on sale.

WARNING: OBSTACLE AHEAD!

Sentimental items may provide a stumbling block. You may have a collection of favors from past special occasions that fill your shelves. And while you cherish the memories associated with them, you're ready to part with the clutter. I have had folks express their fear in getting rid of such sentimental items, that they are afraid they will lose their happy memories and need an item to find their way back to them. You can rest knowing that you have those memories in your heart and can write down what that item means to you now. As you curate sentimental items, take action steps to share the stories with your family members and friends in letter form or book format. Schedule a story time for the future, take a photo of the item, and be free to donate or otherwise release it when you're ready. See page 184 for creative places to donate items.

Step 3: Deliver/Sell/Donate

Delivering items in a small space is easier since you don't need to walk as far! However, storing items that need to be sold can be a real challenge. You may find that donating is a better option. Find a charity that offers a receipt so you can declare the actual cash value of the item for a possible deduction. Donating items to charities that you believe in can help make the decision easier. I chose a charity that provided job training in my community. I met the director and, after 560-plus bags donated, she and I became friends.

Look for space-saving options. Use Shaker-style peg hooks in the entryway. Use small furniture pieces with drawers. Think in terms of unusual pairings; you can use an entryway desk for socks or gloves or for the more traditional purpose of sorting mail and paying bills. Look at awkward corners or "dead space" as opportunities for creative storage with open shelves that can utilize space toward the ceiling. Group like-colored items together even if they're not traditionally used together. My white kitchen plates looked great stored on shelves next to my great-grandmother's white painter's palette. Don't conform to "rules"—store things underneath couches, beds, and chairs. Just use matching storage containers if you don't have a couch cover or bed skirt.

MONEY-SAVING TIP:

Use low-cost, color-coordinated contact paper to cover cardboard boxes for decorative storage. When moving, you'll likely not need to purchase moving boxes, and if they do need to be replaced, you can source boxes from local stores for free and recycle the old ones.

Step 4: Tracking and Celebrating

The tracking step is an opportunity to gather data that can support your journey, but you don't need to be a slave to tracking. It's a useful tool but not a hard-and-fast rule. Remember to keep your Decluttering Chart (page 173) handy. Marking an X for each item eliminated on this chart of squares is a fun and inspiring way to track the decluttering progress. We set an initial goal of 500 items. Never did I dream it would grow to two-thirds of everything we owned being donated, so I recommend that you take it in small increments. Celebrations can be equally incremental. Perhaps having company over in a studio apartment is not what you desire. Can you host a party at a local eatery or park? What about inviting a friend for a long walk through your city? Sharing your journey makes the tracking fun and encourages connection with people rather than stuff.

Saying Goodbye to Stuff

An increasing market exists for space-saving gadgets. As you release items to charity, you will simultaneously release the pressure to obtain more items to solve small-space problems. If you eliminate what you don't need, then you won't need these space-saving gadgets either. You may feel anxious in letting go of items that you've kept "just in case." I recommend writing out your thoughts regarding what you would do in the worst-case scenario. Often, I have not logically thought through my "just in case" fears. In the end, my worst-case scenarios were not likely and were also solvable. As you weigh benefits versus drawbacks, be honest with yourself. Can your small-space considerations lead to greater cooperation with your neighbors or family? Can you offer to share items in your apartment building in a tool-lending co-op? Begin to see the hidden solutions around you!

Own Less, Live More

Look at the exercise of processing the contents of your small space not as downsizing but as curating. Starting with the idea of a blank canvas on which to create will give you the vision to determine what your space will contain. Yes, the dimensions will obviously provide constraints, but you bring your own autonomy and personal responsibility to create in this space. It can be a relief to get complete freedom to define what a home "should" contain and not go with the cultural preconceived notions of what a house should hold. Choose what works best for you!

The benefits of living in a small space include a cozy atmosphere. I also believe that living in a smaller space encourages more time outdoors. And naturally, more time spent outside provides increased vitamin D from sunshine. Look for activities that can help you live more fully as part of your neighborhood, town, or city.

Balancing Work and Home

A simpler lifestyle transcends the home. Another place you can review your resources is in the area of your job or business. Trading time for money is the essence of employment or self-employment; however, when you choose to discard things that don't serve you, you may find renewed interests beyond the nine-to-five grind. Knowing that each item and the space that you must provide for it costs you time and effort at your job will invariably help you make strategic decisions about what you want to spend your life doing. Can you choose to expand your career through additional education ▶

> or networking in the evenings once you have completed your decluttering goal? Would your business be expanded if you had more time and mental energy to give instead of feeling drained by a cluttered apartment? Use these ideas as motivation to keep the benefits of your streamlining goals front and center.

Attachment & Sentiment

Small spaces may help simplify decisions, but they can also amplify emotions due to the transitions that may have factored into your current square footage living situation. This exercise can be insightful as you process your journey.

Feelings Checklist

As you sort through your studio apartment, you may experience a wide variety of emotions:

- **Pleasure** at the simplicity of your options
- **Shame or unhappiness** in having to downsize
- **Pride**
- **Exhaustion**
- **Epiphany** at how much your square footage costs per month
- **Mentally taxed** at the sheer number of decisions that must be made
- **Relief**

- **Gratitude**
- **Nostalgia**
- **Excitement**
- **Appreciation** for the space that you have

These emotions may be particularly complex if you moved to a smaller space against your personal preference. Perhaps a job change or a medical event made the decision for you. Maybe a relationship that ended caused this move. Give yourself grace and allow the feelings to flow onto the pages of your journal.

Reimagining Your Space

Regardless of why you've chosen to live in a small space, your perspective can make all the difference. After one client made a sudden move across the country to escape an abusive relationship, she surprised me with an amazingly positive outlook. "How many other people get a chance like this? To be able to completely start over is a gift!" she told me. Her resilience inspires me still. It's time to reimagine this gift of living in a small space!

Picture Your Perfect Room

My favorite website for design of small spaces is Apartmenttherapy .com. If you are a visual learner, this site is the place to go for studio inspiration. As you identify your learning style, you'll want to start reimagining your space. Are you an auditory learner? Talk through what you want to create with your partner or best friend. Then, after the joy of dreaming together, you'll be able to create your vision board on Pinterest. Do you have a galley-style kitchen? Search for photos of that kind of kitchen setup. Kinesthetic learners who enjoy textures and movement may want to walk through your favorite retail home store or craft store and touch the fabrics until you find the right one. Even if you are predominantly one type of learner, use all your senses. Your vision may progress and change.

Set a target budget next, after you get your vision—not before! Once you can see in your mind what you want, you'll find creative ways to achieve the look and stay under budget. Search the other chapters for Money-Saving Tips. Look at items that can be multipurposed or repurposed. You may enjoy using Visualstager.com, which allows you to upload a photo of your small space and insert digital staging elements. You can purchase a low-cost amount of credits and then use them to choose items similar to what you already own. There are no shopping links associated with these staging items, and that's why I recommend this site before other types of "shop the look" type of sites.

New Uses for New Spaces

As you consider the open spaces you've created, you may want to look for new uses for the space. One of my clients transformed her newly cleared enclosed porch into a reading space for her daughter. Another client changed her home office space into a school space for her children. Still another family found that they could partition off a landing area and create a whole new sleeping space. What opportunities does your newfound space afford?

Measure twice and move furniture once. Look out for awkward corners and additional inches required by trim around doorways. Draw out your floor plan of the room, noting windows, doorways, and heating elements.

When you host guests, keep things small and simple by serving finger food, or opt for different venues close to home for entertaining larger groups. We recently hosted a family of seven from Guam, and I was nervous with our family of eight plus their seven, equaling 15 people in 1,400 square feet. We chose simple meals and spent time at an outdoor park. Our minimalist systems held even in hosting, and yours can, too! Use your creativity in utilizing your newly opened space to accomplish unusual acts of hospitality.

Style & Design

More than any other type of housing, small spaces benefit from a consistent theme. Using a color family with a neutral base color will help to create visual stability.

Small-space strategies abound! Mirrors are an asset that can be used to increase the visual continuity of a small space. Make sure you like the angle and scene in the mirror from different vantage points. Use screens, bookcases, large plants, curtains with ceiling-mounted curtain brackets, or wardrobes to separate zones. Consider the direction the windows face. The direction of light is important in studios or apartments because they don't have windows in all four directions like a stand-alone house.

Ask the landlord first what changes are permitted in apartments that you don't own. That being said, if you pay rent on time and keep the place clean, a landlord may allow you to take doors off, pull up old carpet, and even paint. Remember, if you take off doors then you will need to put them back when you move, and you may need to store the door and hardware in the interim.

If you are considering downsizing into a studio or small living space, look for an open layout, access to nature space, and tall ceilings (although watch for high utilities), and avoid awkward features that sometimes come with older buildings that are modified into apartments.

NINE

Minimalism for Life

"What I know for sure is
you become what you believe."

—OPRAH WINFREY

When I was first introduced to minimalism, I had no idea how far the principles would take me. Maybe as you look back at all that you've accomplished in the previous chapters and rooms, you feel that same sense of awe.

What Does Minimalism Mean for You?

Remember your "before" photo of your entryway, bath, and closets? Can you see the progress? I'm not talking about unrealistic perfection, as any house is a forever work in progress, but it's time to acknowledge and congratulate yourself for the hard work and progress you've made in your thinking and in your life. It might be fun to post some of your "before and after" photos on social media, but be careful to find the affirming worth of your journey in your own soul, regardless of what family or friends or online strangers say. Walk through your home. Own your accomplishment! You've completed a labor of love, for yourself and for those who dwell in or visit your home.

Maybe you've decluttered not out of choice but out of necessity. Any number of life transitions can necessitate a decluttering journey. Now is the time to see the good that can grow during those transitions. Embrace the wisdom your journey has given you. Take a moment to journal about the story of your home in this season, where you have created new routines and redesigned spaces.

You will likely find that you are creating your own personal definition of what minimalism is for you. You may find that a minimalist lifestyle looks completely different from what you thought when you donated your first bag or sold your first item. Perhaps you changed decor styles entirely. On the other side, perhaps minimalism in your home looks remarkably similar to your old life except more authentic and streamlined, showcasing your long-loved masterpieces without the distraction of clutter. Whatever style changes you've made, you are able to now enjoy a more thoughtful, intentional design that is consistent throughout your house and your personal sense of beauty with "less."

With a healthier relationship to items both practical and sentimental, you'll find that you have new skills, new routines, new priorities, new clarity, and new healing that will strengthen you for life ahead. You've grown. You're different, more mindful of the choices that impact your home and world. Perhaps you've always had a pulse on your home, but now you'll truly be in sync with decisions that impact it.

Now is the time to celebrate small and large victories. I certainly did the day I realized I could find my purse and I consistently had money in it! Celebrate the large victories that may not be visible, such as those bonding moments with your child as they conquer math in their newly simplified space. Don't forget to cherish the closeness and unity you created with your partner in your peaceful new master bedroom. Waking up to a clean and simplified kitchen is still a joy I don't take for granted; it's a priceless gift that I gave myself when I decided to give all the clutter away.

I never knew the benefits would continue far into the future when I came to the end of my main decluttering journey, but the benefits continue to grow with each passing year. Instead of a messier house as the days turn into years, I gain further insight into what works best for my family and find simple solutions as the needs of my household change. Decluttering is something you can complete in one sense, but like any worthwhile change, it will require maintenance and attending to. Decluttering should also be the beginning of intentionally crafting your life. Once all the clutter is cleared away, you are free to re-create what you want the rest of your life to look like.

Living Mindfully

When I cleared away the mountains of clutter and its accompanying debilitating mental fog, I made more intentional, more mindful choices about how I spent my time and money. The decluttering journey took a tremendous amount of time and effort. I resented the time away from my children that clutter demanded, and I was determined not to allow clutter to control how I spent my time again. Whenever I thought of those 560-plus bags, I found renewed energy and motivation at night to clear that one last project away. I discovered self-discipline to shut off mindless online surfing and instead focus on new topics that I mindfully chose in order to move my life and businesses forward. I remembered the countless hours sorting boxes in the basement and vowed I would never go back to allowing clutter to pile up.

This is the progression I now go through when considering a purchase:

1. Can I solve this problem myself or fix what I have?

2. Do I have something else that will also work instead of this worn/broken item?

3. Can I borrow the item needed for a single task?

4. Can I trade something for it?

5. Can I rent it?

6. Can I live without it?

7. Can I delay purchasing it until I have more time to think of a solution?

I also set myself up for success by setting a regular decluttering day, usually once per month. This decluttering day covers the whole house since we've already decluttered so much and now only need to spot-check. However, you may find that if your family works together in decluttering spaces, everyone will start practicing these new skills as part of normal everyday living. This will help make your monthly decluttering day easier and easier.

You may not realize how much others are watching and learning from you. Recently, my 10-year-old announced, "Mom, I need to declutter my school shelf so I can find things. I have too many papers." After a quick sort of his school shelf, my son and I went for a run together on our country road. He initiated the decluttering and also the reward. Priceless! Keep choosing appropriate rewards each time you declutter.

Sustainability

Now that you have new routines for decluttering, you may have also found that sustainable choices have become your normal routine. Be sensitive, too, that not everyone will share your same convictions toward sustainable living right away. You may want to review the Sustainability Tips throughout previous chapters as you discuss ways to work together toward better environmental stewardship. Environmental stewardship is a process. No one is grading you, and you're free to enjoy the creativity of constant improvement. Because this lifestyle aligns with your core values, as you stay on track, your friends and family will naturally learn from you and want to join your passion. One of the ways you can ensure that you don't fall back into consumption habits is to make it easy for yourself to practice zero-waste routines. Always set your future self up for success by making recycling convenient, placing bulk zero-waste supplies on auto ship, and sharing your views respectfully with others. The more I talked about "green living," the more I found encouragement from others interested in making those same changes.

Community brings encouragement and innovation, too. Join local groups or start one focused on environmental stewardship. Become a lifelong learner on topics of conservation and local wildlife and plant life. Choose to decorate with flowers and use plants from outside your door rather than buying fake plastic greenery. When you have the urge to go shopping just to shop, shift to "shop" in nature by visiting local parks for photo opportunities. A simple sunset is more stunning than anything in the mall. Being mindful of the environment can bring new habits that break the need to consume and accumulate physical items and instead begin to gather beautiful memories. The more that you surround yourself with environmentally sound choices, the more those choices become automatic.

The Minimalist Way of Life

Like running a marathon, the minimalist way of life is accomplished one foot in front of the other. Step by step, room by room, you've accomplished a monumental task! With each space or room, you're seeing the freedom in creating systems, solving problems, and building stronger bonds with those you love. You're likely seeing renewed passion for simple and sustainable living, and that daily commitment brings deep satisfaction. I hope you hear my voice cheering you on!

Remember how big the task seemed at the beginning? The laundry mountain or the enormous pile of papers and bills was probably alarming, but look at all that you've conquered. You should feel deep satisfaction at the amount of journaling, sorting, donating, and prioritizing you've done to re-create your home in order for it to serve you.

When I close my eyes, I see my beloved clients who conquered significant literal and figurative mountains by decluttering their lives. One mom has cleared the clutter that was feeding her depression and suicidal thoughts. Today, she's able to be more mindful and present with raising her kids. A military wife is not tripping over toys as she plans for her husband's next deployment. Their relationship is restored, having better communication helped them to eliminate divorce papers, and their sweet family is stronger than it was when she started donating to charity. A different client decluttered her residence and negative emotions from an abusive relationship. She recently took a job working from home, eliminating a grueling commute and providing a fresh new start. These are just a few examples of how living mindfully becomes second nature and new choices bring new opportunities.

As you reach the goal you set for yourself in the beginning of this book, you may have the feeling of "What's next?" I know that I felt a bit nervous and excited when I reached that mountaintop of completing a whole house (and life!) decluttering.

Maybe you feel a sting of shame at having a clean and beautiful home. I know that I didn't feel worthy of having a home that I was proud of. Even as I write this, I feel the irony that I am writing a book on minimalism and have worked with private clients all over the globe to simplify their homes. You should have seen my basement when I first began; I would've been voted least likely to succeed, there was so much junk! Yet choosing to believe and to relentlessly create sacred space brought me here, writing to you. If you struggle to feel worthy, know that you *are* worthy.

Perhaps you thought you'd never get to the top of this decluttering "mountain" you had to climb and feel a bit of fear in anticipation of the future. Let that fear turn to awe as you look beyond this mountain toward a new dream. How will you spend your time now? A new dream may become visible now that you've simplified your life enough to see it.

The minimalist way of life is not about continual decluttering; the binge-and-purge pattern is not a lifelong cycle. Far from it! Minimalism is a foundation, a humble beginning in the exciting journey of creating your best, most intentional life. Here you stand, ready now to begin anew. Free. Focused. Self-disciplined and owning your life.

Minimalism may be for you, as it was for me, a new beginning of an entirely new life with new opportunities and possibilities that I had only dreamed about a few short years ago. So where are you headed next? Wherever you choose, keep going, keep growing, keep climbing! Embrace your next season with gratitude. And, dear friend, blessings for your journey.

Decluttering Chart

1. Keep a representative of sets; donate the rest.

2. Donate to causes you believe strongly in supporting.

3. Take a photo and create a photo book filled with pictures and add text.

4. Write a story about the item and the feelings behind it, add the photos, and create an e-book to share with future generations.

5. Share the item with another family member or friend. (Always ask permission first and be ready to graciously accept that they may decline your offer. Don't share if you would have your feelings hurt if they didn't want it or take care of it to the level you'd expect.)

6. Consider the time frame from when you received the sentimental item. Has it been long enough for you to have enjoyed it? Do you still enjoy it?

7. Recycle or repurpose the item into something that you can use daily and enjoy.

I don't recommend selling these items unless the monetary value is substantial to your budget. The money simply isn't ever going to be worth it.

Instructions: Put an X in each box for every item or bag that you donate/trash/share. You can find additional copies of this chart on callistomediabooks.com/minimalismroombyroom.

Set a goal (there are 500 squares here) with a reward at the end.

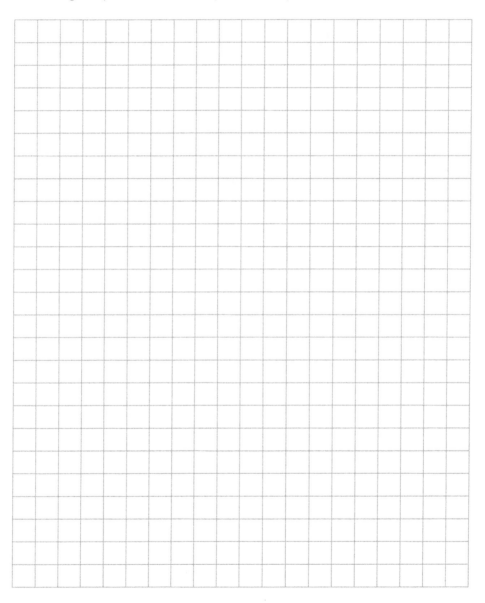

REWARD: _____

Post this chart on the back of rooms as you move through your home and spaces.

Attach a photo of your reward. For example, attach a picture of the ocean if you're headed to the beach with money from items sold.

Annual Calendar Sheet for Annual/Biannual Expenses

Write the name of the expense and due date in the space provided. Then calculate what you need to save each pay cycle for that bill. You can find additional copies of this expense sheet on callistomedia books.com/minimalismroombyroom.

Items due in January _____

_____

_____

Items due in February _____

_____

_____

Items due in March _____

_____

_____

Items due in April _____

_____

_____

Items due in May _____

_____

_____

Items due in June

Items due in July

Items due in August

Items due in September

Items due in October

Items due in November

Items due in December

Tracking Sheet for Items to Sell

You can find additional copies of this tracking sheet on callistomedia books.com/minimalismroombyroom.

NAME OF ITEM	ASKING PRICE	DATE LISTED FB MARKET-PLACE	DATE LISTED CRAIGSLIST	DATE LISTED BUY/SELL/TRADE GROUP	GARAGE SALE	SOLD PRICES
Example: Bookshelves	$50.00	9-1-19	9-2-19	9-2-19	n/a	$45.00

Total Amount Toward Reward: _____

How to Design a Child's Capsule Wardrobe

This will be a living document and will need frequent updates. You can find additional copies of this chart on callistomediabooks.com/minimalismroombyroom. You'll want to have one copy of each sheet for each child.

I recommend having a set annual amount and then dividing it into a monthly amount.

For example: $120 per child per year works out to be $10 per month. You won't spend that each month, but it helps to visualize the amount needed.

AMOUNT NEEDED	ITEM	SIZE	PREFERRED BRAND	LOCATION TO FIND	ITEM PRICE	ANNUAL BUDGET	MONTHLY AMOUNT
	Winter Needs						
1	Hats				$5.00		
1	Gloves			Thrift Store	$5.00		
1	Coats			eBay	$50.00		
5	Winter shirts				$25.00		
5	Pants		Dickies brand with reinforced knees		$25.00		
3	Sweaters						
	Summer Needs						
1	Swimsuit				$10.00		
5	Summer shirts						
5	Short/skirts						
	Sports Clothing						
1-2	Uniforms						
3	Practice						
	Formal Attire						
2	Button-down shirts						
2	Slacks						
	Dresses/skirts						
	Shoes						
1	Adventure shoes / Running shoes		Merrill brand				

AMOUNT NEEDED	ITEM	SIZE	PREFERRED BRAND	LOCATION TO FIND	ITEM PRICE	ANNUAL BUDGET	MONTHLY AMOUNT
1	Rain boots		Kamik *long-lasting and you can send them back when they are worn out for Kamik to recycle them.				
1	Formal shoes						
6 pairs	Socks						
	Underclothes						
6-9 pairs	Age-appropriate sleepwear						
Total Amount					$120.00	$120.00	$10.00

AMOUNT NEEDED	ITEM	SIZE	PREFERRED BRAND	LOCATION TO FIND	ITEM PRICE	ANNUAL BUDGET	MONTHLY AMOUNT
Winter Needs							
Summer Needs							
Sports Clothing							
Formal Attire							
Shoes							

AMOUNT NEEDED	ITEM	SIZE	PREFERRED BRAND	LOCATION TO FIND	ITEM PRICE	ANNUAL BUDGET	MONTHLY AMOUNT
Underclothes							

Creative Places to Donate

Local Public, Private, and Montessori Schools

Day Care Centers

Senior Centers

Nursing Homes

Homeless Shelters

Veterans Homes and Hospitals

County Human Services Departments

Women's Domestic Violence Shelters

St. Vincent de Paul Society

Salvation Army

Humane Society or Animal Shelters

Doctor's Offices (for magazines, periodicals, and some books)

Community Health Clinics

Food Pantries

High School Drama Departments or Local Actors Guilds (for theatrical props)

Photographers (for props, costumes, vintage furniture, candles)

Religious Organizations that provide "Free Store" donation days to the poor

Running Stores (many receive shoes for Nike's Reuse-a-Shoe program: purpose.nike.com/reuse-a-shoe)

Resources

Chapter 1 The Minimalist Lifestyle

Online Resources as You Get Started Decluttering

www.createminimalism.com

alliecasazza.com/start-here

zenhabits.net

www.theminimalists.com

www.becomingminimalist.com

Chapter 2 Entryway, Bathrooms, and Communal Closets

Online Photos Design Inspiration

www.pinterest.com/ejphillips22/design-inspiration

www.instagram.com/generalstore

www.kinfolk.com

www.instagram.com/the.minimalist.kin

Books for Starting Your Minimalist Journey

Kinfolk books/magazines

Zero Waste Home by Bea Johnson

Homebody by Joanna Gaines

Online Blogs for Design Tips

zerowastehome.com/about/photos

nourishingminimalism.com

leanneford.com/projects

magnolia.com/blog

thenester.com

decordemon.blogspot.com/search/label/DESIGN

Frugal Minimalist Facebook Group: www.facebook.com/groups/1421204557930992

Chapter 3 The Home Office

Overcoming Hard Emotions in the Area of Finances

Better Than You Feel by Drenda Keesee

Fixing the Money Thing by Gary Keesee

Online Photos of Minimalist Office Design

www.pinterest.com/ejphillips22/design-inspiration

www.instagram.com/p/BxcgwlOlelM

www.instagram.com/explore/tags/minimalistoffice

Tech Tools for Office Simplicity

www.neat.com

www.trello.com

docs.google.com/spreadsheets

docs.google.com/document

Chapter 4 Kids' Bedrooms and Playrooms

Fun Resources to Involve Your Children in the Decluttering/ Design Process

Homemade zero-waste paint recipe: www.vermints.com/blog/make-natural -paint-with-leftover-fruits-and-veggies

Last Child in the Woods by Richard Louv

Marie Kondo's guide to folding: www.youtube.com/watch?v=vAme97fLUsw

Life at Home in the 21st Century: www.youtube.com/watch?v=3AhSNsBs2YO

jamesmollison.com/books/where-children-sleep

www.homeadvisor.com/r/home-energy-conservation-for-kids

Books for Help with Conversations with Kids

Calming Angry Kids by Tricia Goyer

Personality Plus for Parents by Florence Littauer

Chapter 5 Living and Family Rooms

Online Resources to Help with Design and Photo Inspiration

thenester.com

www.myscandinavianhome.com

www.remodelista.com

www.decordemon.blogspot.com

leanneford.com/projects

Books with Tips and Strategies for Designing Living Spaces

The Nesting Place by Myquillyn Smith

Abode by Serena Mitnik-Miller and Mason St. Peter

Homebody by Joanna Gaines

Cozy Minimalist Home by Myquillyn Smith

Chapter 6 Kitchen and Dining Areas

Online Resources for Simplicity in the Kitchen

www.theminimalists.com/packing

www.blisshaus.com

www.zerowastehome.com

Books for Organizing the Kitchen

Home Management: Plain & Simple by Kim Brenneman

Keeping House by Margaret Kim Peterson

Chapter 7 The Master Bedroom

Online Resources for Design Inspiration

theinspiredroom.net/2013/02/14/fall-in-love-with-your-home

www.houzz.com

poshmark.com

www.thredup.com

www.huffpost.com/entry/10-tips-to-create-a-peaceful
-bedroom_b_57d2de2fe4b0f831f7071bac

Books for Decluttering Ideas, Creating Cleaning Products, and Building Healthy Communication

Love & Respect by Emerson Eggerichs

Green this! Volume 1: Greening Your Cleaning by Deirdre Imus

Hidden Solutions All Around You by Daniel R. Castro

Keeping House by Margaret Kim Peterson

Online Resources for Clothing Decluttering

classyyettrendy.com/2017/02/start-capsule-wardrobe-5-steps.html

zerowastehome.com/2012/10/10/50-ways-to-wear-mens-shirt-i-did-i

Chapter 8 Studio Apartments and Other Small Spaces

Online Resources for Small-Space Design

visualstager.com

www.apartmenttherapy.com/moving-checklist-what-to-do-before-downsizing
-to-a-studio-225954

www.apartmenttherapy.com/learning-to-go-with-the-flow-while-making-you
r-room-a-nicer-place-to-be-the-style-cure-assignment-14-211982

thenoshery.com/tips-downsizing-to-a-tiny-house

smallspacebigtaste.co

www.huffpost.com/entry/7-awesome-benefits-to-small-space-living
_b_5790fa7ae4b0a9208b5f2e16

www.apartmenttherapy.com/small-apartment-real-estate-tips-36633450

Chapter 9 Minimalism for Life

Books for Dreaming Up Your Next Steps Now That You're a Minimalist

The Magic of Thinking Big by David J Schwartz, PhD

The Dream Giver by Bruce Wilkinson

Index

Acknowledgments

My deepest thanks and appreciation extend to the following:

To Claire Yee and all the editorial team, thank you for your relentless edits and keen eye for details.

To my children, Andrea, Nathan, Ethan, William, Brenan, and Kenan, for running the household smoothly while I was writing. You are my inspiration.

To Michael Enright, Denise Enright, Mary Calderhead, Jessica Kay Kruse, and all my beloved family and friends for your loyalty, prayers, and tireless assistance.

To my Frugal Minimalist FB admin/moderator team and all 89,000+ members. You inspire me every day to never give up sharing the benefits of minimalism.

To my private clients. You have always been a joy to serve.

To Kurt. You believed in me.

Always to God. You told me to get my house in order and gave me the strength to do it.

About the Author

Elizabeth Enright Phillips is a professional financial and minimalist coach serving clients locally in Ohio and online. She supports her clients in their decluttering journey through individual and group coaching focused on creating simplicity in the home and stability in the finances. She blogs about money-saving and minimalist strategies at createminimalism.com. She can be reached at elizabeth@createminimalism.com.

CPSIA information can be obtained
at www.ICGtesting.com
Printed in the USA
BVHW091857270520
580327BV00003B/27